Those who came forward

Those who came forward

Men and women
who responded to
the ministry of Billy Graham

by Curtis Mitchell

Preface by
Dr. Billy Graham

Chilton Books
A Division of Chilton Company
Publishers
Philadelphia and New York

"I say unto you, that even so there shall be joy in heaven over one sinner that repenteth, more than over ninety and nine righteous persons who need no repentence."

—LUKE 15:7

Preface by
Dr. Billy Graham

Just seventeen years ago, my evangelistic work came to the attention of the public as the result of a crusade in Los Angeles, California.

As I have said many times, it was like a bolt from the blue. I was bewildered, challenged, and humbled. I was bewildered because I had no formal theological training. I was challenged because I saw new doors of opportunity swinging wide. I was humbled because it seemed that God was laying His hand on the most unlikely prospect among His servants for a gigantic task.

Since that beginning, we have traveled to every continent to bring to countless millions the good news of Jesus Christ and His Resurrection. In taking each new step, we have tried to follow His leading, and to God we give all the glory.

Now a writer and a friend, Curtis Mitchell, has written a work called *Those Who Came For-*

ward, which is a study of the experiences of some of the thousands who have responded to the invitation to accept Jesus Christ as given in our crusades and through radio and television.

As he knows, I would prefer that my ministry be documented only after it is finished, when it might be most accurately assessed. However, I respect his conviction that a closer look now at the quality of change made in the lives of new Christians in the aftermath of their conversions might be both enlightening and inspiring.

Certainly, Mr. Mitchell has enjoyed a unique opportunity to observe our work. He has followed many of our crusades and sat in our press box night after night. He has interviewed many of those whose lives have been changed as a result of attending our meetings and surrendering themselves to Jesus Christ. I know also that he is deeply concerned about the Christian steadfastness of young people who are oftentimes joining our churches today without adequate preparation or understanding of God's plan of salvation.

So I applaud his intention of clarifying and illuminating, through the lives of the persons about whom he writes, the steps to personal commitment.

It *is* true that lives are sermons, or should be, and I pray that the experiences here presented will help to bring men to find the same Christ who changed the lives of others, and so to assist them to discover their own destiny in God's great Kingdom.

BILLY GRAHAM
Montreat

Foreword

The solid-looking citizen seated beside me in the transcontinental airplane motioned abruptly toward the magazine I was reading. "That man changed my life," he said.

I had been leafing through "Decision" magazine, the publication of the Billy Graham Evangelistic Association, which goes to more than three million readers each month.

"What man?" I asked.

"Billy Graham," he said. "I went forward during his crusade in New York in 1957."

I have written stories about the evangelist for more than a decade. Inevitably, I have met many persons who have responded to his invitation. Again and again, I have been caught up in the wonderfulness of what has happened to so many of them. All told, those who have come forward in his meetings must total by now more than one million souls.

The man went on: "I enrolled in a college that fall and got my degree, and then went to a seminary. It was rough, I tell you. Now I'm a pastor of a church on the West Coast."

"What were you before?" I asked.

He grinned at the memory. "I was a no-good, played-out bellhop in a cheap hotel," he said.

What finally happens to people who come forward in a Billy Graham crusade? The question is asked year after year. My seat-mate was part of the answer.

Some years ago, I attacked the mystery. For a long time, researchers had been busy in behalf of this newspaper or that, or working for this group or the other. They offered me head counts, often contradictory: so many persons who had professed interest, so many who had joined a particular church, so many who fell away. Then I found that social workers had tried out their most sensitive sociometric measurements, probing depth of experience, and trying to average it out. They all failed. Not one, neither scientist nor mathematician, could measure the essence of the conversion experience which, by its nature, was as unique as the individual who professed it.

So I turned ultimately to the oldest research technique known to history, which is reporting a story about a fellow human being, and then moving on to another and another. The method assures depth as well as integrity for the record of the individuals concerned. So hereafter in these pages is my own survey of some of those who came forward, and whose selflessness and love of God and man can be extrapolated, I believe, to countless others. I cannot prove this statement, but I assert that it is true.

At any rate, here are stories of human inquirers who came forward in crusades held from five to ten years ago and who today constitute a valorous battalion of veterans who march to the music of "Onward, Christian Soldiers!" And here also are letters from many others, needy men and women and young people recruited more recently by Billy Graham's international crusades, his "Hour of Decision" on radio, his TV telecasts, and his association's publications.

To all of them, each of whom is a hero or heroine in this work, I am grateful that their example has given me the opportunity of attesting to a modern Pentecost.

In particular, I acknowledge my indebtedness to many members of the Billy Graham Team who gave me much of their time and wisdom; to Sherwood Wirt, editor of "Decision" magazine, wherein some of these lives and letters have already been chronicled; to Robert O. Ferm, who told a parallel tale in his earlier book, *Persuaded to Live,* and whose encouragement guided my early efforts; to George M. Wilson, executive vice-president of the Billy Graham Evangelistic Association; and, finally and gratefully, to Billy Graham himself.

CURTIS MITCHELL
Westport, Connecticut

Contents

Part One: 1
   Why they came forward

Part Two: 53
   Their lives

Part Three: 235
   Their letters

Part One

Why they came forward

"Jesus made everything so simple and we have made it so complicated . . . All you can do is call upon God to 'turn' you."

BILLY GRAHAM

Conversion as Billy Graham sees it

A PERSONAL EXPERIENCE, A CONVER-
SION IS THE GIFT BILLY GRAHAM
SEEKS FOR ALL, SO THAT MAN'S
HEART CAN BE CHANGED, AND THEN
THE WHOLE WORLD.

"Every public servant
is tallest on his knees."

LYNDON B. JOHNSON

On Sunday afternoon, November 28, 1965, Billy Graham became the first evangelist in history to have in his audience a President of the United States.

His subject was "The Great Judgment Day."

His plea was that men would turn from prejudice, pride, lust, greed, jealousy, and hatred to a new dimension of living to be found in the person of Jesus Christ.

Sitting in a private box tucked under the amazing roof of the Houston, Texas, Astrodome, a sober-faced President Johnson and his First Lady saw every seat in the rainbow-hued bowl filled, and an overflow of thousands spilling out across the green plastic grass of the infield. Centered above second base, a man-high platform held chairs for a hundred distinguished visitors and Billy Graham's pulpit.

Speaking directly to President Lyndon B. Johnson, Graham pledged the prayers of his audience "that God will continue to grant you wisdom, strength and courage for the overwhelming responsibilities that you bear."

Addressing the crowd of 61,000 persons, unprecedented in the Astrodome, he told them, "It was the President's great-grandfather who helped Sam Houston find a personal experience with Jesus Christ, a conversion that not only changed the life of that great Texan, but which influences religious life in Texas today."

A personal experience! A conversion!

These are troublesome words, but key words. Persons outside the Christian faith rarely understand them. Even some individuals within the Church fail to comprehend their significance. Yet, they are crucial to the process by which the human being becomes a child of God and a member of His Kingdom.

What is a "personal experience"? What does "conversion" do to people? We shall see!

In their lofty Astrodome box, the President and his First Lady heard Graham conclude his sermon and then ask his audience to let Christ come into their lives. The organ played a muted hymn, "Just As I Am." The evangelist's invitation was urgent, couched in simple, easily understood phrases:

"You are not living the right kind of life unless Christ is first. I'm asking you to make that great commitment. I'm asking you by faith to come to His cross where He shed His blood for you and let Him clean up your past, change your life, and make you a new person."

They sensed rather than saw the initial response among the rapt audience, and almost at once they could

4

discern distant figures making their way into the aisles. At first, they were a thin trickle down the passageways, and then the stream widened and became a torrent gushing down every stadium slope, curving around stanchions, bouncing off blocks of seats, but always moving until it reached the open space of the infield before Billy Graham's platform.

Finally, the flood ceased and the closely packed mass stood silent, with faces upturned, waiting. Graham led them through a short prayer of repentance and confession. They repeated it, two thousand voices so soft they could hardly be heard. Then, as Graham turned to depart, the battalions of converts changed into a new formation, presenting an amazing picture. The solid mass divided suddenly into twosomes and threesomes, each a private entity. Some people lounged, some sat crosslegged on the grass, but all were suddenly engaged in serious, person-to-person talk. A youth in an Ivy league suit confronted a teenager in Texas boots. A lady in a sweater sat beside a woman in a mink stole, a Negro minister counseled a tanned rancher; a matron knelt before a trio of children of three races.

The First Lady, watching attentively, drew a deep breath. What mystical experience had lifted those hundreds from their seats? What was the meaning of their clear eyes and uplifted faces? What emotions and what sensations rioted within each breast?

Answers to such queries have come from persons who were converted in earlier crusades and whose faith has endured year after year.

Mabel L. Duvall, government worker of Washington, D.C., says, "I had the feeling that a hand had been

5

laid on my shoulder and turned me around in a complete about-face."

Rosemary Murphy, of Indiana, a former "Mrs. America" says: "There was a wrenching and a tearing, and then there was a flood of warmth that was overpowering . . . so very much happiness filled me that I did not feel I could contain it all."

Writer Yvonne Simms, of London, says: "When the Holy Spirit entered my heart, He heightened every aspect of life, like a sixth sense."

Jim Percy, formerly a college student in New York, says: "I can never forget the indescribable ecstasy of that moment."

Gertrude Pellman, mother and homemaker, says, "I have a new husband and the children have a new father. What a blessing for a couple to be not only of one flesh but also of one spirit."

Automobile dealer John Hedges, of Indianapolis, says: "I don't see how any man can stay in business and not take Christ along with him."

Dr. Nelles Silverthorne, pediatrician of Canada, says: "As a man of science, I am sure. It (conversion) is the most convincing experiment I've ever done."

Chef Heintz Pellman, of Germany and Canada, says: "My heart was filled with love for all the world. My former race prejudice melted away."

Youth counselor and war hero Louis Zamperini, of Los Angeles, says: "I realized there was some reason God had spared my life in that wartime plane crash and then in the prisoner-of-war camps. I also felt that God had allowed my long siege of hard luck to bring me to Him."

Such joyous hallelujahs make a happy sound against

the background of today's cacophony of doom. It is a sound the world needs because the air is filled with the racket of protesting recalcitrants, the sirens of ambulances, fire trucks, and police cruisers, and the distant thud of high explosives landing on jungle battlegrounds. And everywhere, the man on the street, as well as the highest ranking political potentate, goes about his business waiting for the other shoe to drop.

Graham asserts, "It seems that the demons of hell have been let loose. The fires of passion, hate, greed, and lust are sweeping over the world and we seem to be plunging toward Armageddon. This is the tormented generation, this is the generation destined to live in the midst of crisis, fear, and death. We are like a people under the sentence of death, waiting for the date of execution to be set. We sense that something is about to happen. We know that things cannot go on as they are. History seems to have reached an impasse. We are on a collision course. Something is about to give, and all of mankind is crying tonight, 'What must I do to be saved?' "

Obviously, the human race is at the end of its tether. It has tried a half-dozen remedies and all have failed.

Education once seemed a hopeful means, until two world wars and the possibility of human extinction through the atomic bomb demonstrated its futility.

Prosperity and well-being once offered a glimmer of hope, and our affluent society burgeoned into the highest standard of living in history, making us the world's richest nation. The result is that we live in a whirlwind of envy, hatred and distrust. Amid all our possessions, we grow ever more selfish and grasping, powerless to change

7

our world. Willy-nilly, we are forced to compete in the economic rat race, aware that such a race is always won by a rat.

Art and culture, it was thought, would inspire men to love of beauty, so our enlightenment has given blind support to whatever might emerge from our geniuses. The result is not reassuring. Today's paintings are paranoid puzzlements, incomprehensible to most. Our literature is a running sewer. Our music is cacophonous, our dancing bestial, reminiscent of the breeding barn rather than the temple.

With the finest health care in the world, our medical science is so fragmented that the whole man is forgotten, with the result that a million persons die annually of cardiovascular disease, which is largely preventable; our hospitals are overwhelmed by a tidal wave of mental illness.

Corruption, double-dealing, and infidelity are so much a way of life in business, in government, and in the home that sins are not even recognized for what they are.

So the lonely human, surrounded by the atmospheric sewage that pollutes his air and the terrestrial sewage that fouls his nest is thrust back upon his own inadequate resources. For a while, he may discover an analgesic in the pursuit of Things, filling his pleasure chest with cars, boats, planes, and beautiful women, exciting his senses with speed and sex, but these are not enough.

He may turn, then, to pills of the sort which spread their multicolored flood across every American city. And these fail, too.

Presently, he takes his hunger and misery to a psychiatrist, who tries to help him toward an adjustment. "Who am I?" he asks. "Do I have any meaning at all?"

"You must see yourself as you are," he is told, and the process of seeing and accepting and adjusting is begun. But the injustice of the family, the corporation, and the government presses too harshly. Ultimately, adjustment is merely another snare. Millions of Germans adjusted to Adolph Hitler, with tragic consequences. Adjustment is to become acceptable to others. What if those others are tyrants and cheats?

Or perhaps the battered bit of human flotsam seeks the refuge of that long sleep called alcoholism.

Having tried everything, what is man to do?

Bishop Sheen reminds us: "A flat tire cannot fix itself."

But there is a way. Catherine Marshall, writing in *Beyond Ourselves,* says,

> Men have demonstrated that they cannot change themselves. Nor can men change other men. We have seen that education does not necessarily achieve it, nor legislation, nor raising incomes, nor plying them with all the gadgets that money can buy. That brings us to the crown of the Holy Spirit's work among men. Only Christ can change human nature, and it is the Holy Spirit that makes Christ available to needy mankind.

Against hopelessness and defeatism, Billy Graham thrusts the dynamic challenge of the Scriptures. "To change the world, you must first change the hearts of men," he says. "You must be born again."

The Bible is his authority—

The Psalmist said, "Then will I teach transgressors thy ways and sinners shall be converted unto thee."

Simon Peter said, "Repent ye, therefore, and be converted, that your sins may be blotted out."

9

And Jesus proclaimed, "Except ye be converted and become as little children, ye shall not enter into the kingdom of heaven."

This is the message to which millions have listened since that seminal crusade held in Los Angeles in 1949 when young Graham, just 31 years old, was projected into the national limelight.

This is the message to which hundreds of thousands have responded in sports stadiums around the world, in playrooms, barrooms, and custom-built parlors lighted only by a TV set, and with surprising frequency, even in Billy Graham's own rumpled hotel suite.

Its essence, so frequently missed in formal church worship, is the simple surrender of all that one *is* in order to partake of the divine nature and *become* all that God, through Jesus Christ, can make one. Readers who have come to this point, and who are not familiar with the terms in which conversion must be couched, are urged to continue through the next chapter where, in Billy Graham's own words, the elements of rebirth and new life are clearly and simply expounded.

The reward will be beyond your expectation. For God, through His revealed word—if you have the faith to believe—has promised amazing treasures. Listen—

Of good things, the Bible says: "The Lord will give grace and glory: no good thing will be withheld from them that walk uprightly."

Of abundant life: "I am come that they might have life, and that they might have it more abundantly."

Of unknowable wonders: "Eye hath not seen, nor ear heard, neither have entered into the heart of man the things which God hath prepared for them that love him."

Of great deeds: "I tell you, he who believes in me

will do the very deeds I do, and still greater deeds than these."

Of strength: "Be not afraid, neither be thou dismayed; for the Lord thy God is with thee, whithersoever thou goest."

Of victory: "If God be for us, who can be against us?"

And this is merely the beginning. The incomparable reward of eternal life, Billy Graham tells his audiences, "begins the moment one invites Jesus Christ into his heart."

And ultimately there is the reality of God's Kingdom wherein He has promised to lay up great stores of treasures against the coming of His children.

The first step is willingness to hear the summons. "Are you willing?"

Graham has driven that question into the hearts and minds of more millions than any evangelist in history. Uncounted thousands have responded.

The First Lady, seeing so many come forward in that last service of the Houston crusade, and recalling that 10,000 others had already joined that penitent band during the week, said, "Wonderful, wonderful! But what happens now?"

The visible aspect of the answer lay before her in the innumerable pairings of converts and trained counselors. The Graham team uses counsel as the first step of what it calls "the follow-up." As conversion may be compared to a new birth, so the follow-up may be compared to the care given by loving parents to a new life. The end result is, hopefully, that each of the newborn will be guided into a Christian fellowship in some organized church. Indeed, this aftercare may make the difference

11

between failure and success. When either an evangelist or a church neglects it, the result can be a calamity.

Many years ago, a teenager came forward during a revival in a midwestern church. He heard a prayer said for his soul, he felt a pat of approval on his thin shoulders, and that was all. The fellowship he sought, the love he yearned for, were denied by church members who were too busy with their own affairs, with holding antique sales and bridge parties and attending lectures. So he left their company and began to make his own way in the world. Presently he became so famous that his name was headlined in every newspaper in the land and his life became the subject of books, television programs, and a Hollywood movie. He was John Dillinger, America's Public Enemy No. 1.

It is never too early; it is never too late.

One is never too innocent or too wicked to escape God's love.

Man's yearning for a higher and better self never ceases. Feed him with Lucullan banquets, dress him in Italian silks and English tweeds, house him in mansions, pour the wealth of oil lands and gold mines into his hands, prime his mind with science, pad his ego with public adulation; in the night's solitude, he will still be a searcher for that which eludes him, and which must always elude him, until he learns the secret of eternal life.

The essence of it all is the death of pride which some call self-love. Dag Hammarskjöld, the late Secretary General of the United Nations, wrote of it in these words:

> I have found [how man should live] in the writings of those great medieval mystics for whom self-surrender has

been the way to self-realization, and who in "singleness of mind" and "inwardness" had found strength to say yes to every demand which the needs of their neighbors made them face. Love . . . for them . . . meant true self-oblivion.

The supreme moral moment of one's life is the human encounter with the person of Jesus Christ, and one's personal surrender to His lordship. This meeting has been compared to two drops of water quivering on a window pane. Each is an entity; each is separate from the other. But suddenly they touch and then—in a twinkling—they are one, indivisible. So with man and God; until man is no longer alone and helpless but is infused with the Holy Spirit. God's promises, from now on, are man's for the claiming.

"Have you been born again?" Graham asks. "Have you been converted?"

From rebirth to the redeeming of God's promises is a long climb up the rocky road called Straight. But thousands have traveled it, and are traveling it today. Their first steps toward righteousness are told in Billy Graham's own words in the next section. Their subsequent guidance is described in Section III.

Of all those who come forward, some are like the seeds that fall on barren ground and are eaten by wild fowl; some encounter a soil too hard to receive their roots; some alight among weeds so thick that their life is choked; but others find glorious nourishment at the hands of skilled husbandmen, and they multiply a hundredfold.

These last are the lives which are reported herein, and which assert positive proof of the reality of God's promises, as you shall see.

An address by Billy Graham

HOW TO TURN ABOUT . . . AND HOW TO RELEASE FROM WITHIN YOURSELF THE POWER OF THE IRRESISTIBLE GOD

"You will develop new strength, climb to new heights, and never know fatigue. The Lord God will give you victory, health, riches, and talents. And you shall not perish but have everlasting life."

—PARAPHRASE OF
ISAIAH 40:31
DEUTERONOMY 30:9
JOHN 3:16

Let us turn to the eighteenth chapter of Matthew's Gospel and the third verse. We will start at the first verse.

"At the same time came the disciples unto Jesus, saying, Who is the greatest in the kingdom of heaven?

"And Jesus called a little child unto him, and set him in the midst of them.

"And said, 'Verily I say unto you, except ye be converted and become as little children, ye shall not enter into the kingdom of heaven.' "

What about this word "conversion"? The disciples came to Jesus and said, "Who is going to be first in your kingdom?" Jesus had already said, "He that will be first must be last."

The requirement for entrance into Heaven is true humility, not a false piety, but a true, genuine humility!

It is the requirement that recognizes our need and our sin and the greatness and the majesty of God, and shows a willingness to receive Christ as Savior.

So, to illustrate the point, Jesus called a little child to Him and said, "Look at this little child, how trusting this little child is, how humble this child is." Before you can get to Heaven you will have to become converted like a little child.

You must go back almost to your childhood, said Jesus. You must trust in God with that same simplicity, that same humility, that same dependence, that a little child has for his parents.

In other words, conversion is simply a change in the direction of your life to a totally different direction.

That is the simple meaning of conversion. It means to turn around. It means to change.

A Chicago psychologist once said, "This generation needs converting more than any generation in history."

A famous British psychologist recently said, "We are so psychologically constituted as to need converting and if the church fails to convert people, we psychologists are going to have to do it." So even psychology is recognizing the need for man to be converted.

The Bible teaches that you must be converted to enter Heaven. The psychiatrist teaches that you must be converted in order to get the most out of life.

The question I want to ask is, Have you been converted to Jesus Christ? Do you know it, are you sure of it? If not, it could happen to you right now.

Conversion is taught all the way through the Bible.

16

Ezekiel 36:26 says this: "A new heart also will I give you, and a new spirit will I put within you: and I will take away the stony heart out of your flesh, and I will give you an heart of flesh."

God is saying through Ezekiel, "I can give you a new heart."

Now the "heart" all the way through the Scriptures stands for the seat of the soul:—your ego, your intelligence, the seat of your emotions is said to be in the heart.

God says, "I'll take out the old heart and put in a new heart." God never patches anybody up. He never does it partially. He always performs a complete process of regeneration.

And conversion means you get a new nature; you get a new heart. Have you received a new nature?

In the Gospel, Jesus calls conversion "being born again," "repenting of sin," "entering a narrow gate," and many other expressions.

Call it anything you like. Call it dedication. Call it surrender. Call it repentance. Call it grace. Call it anything you like.

Have *you* had this encounter with Christ? Peter calls it in Acts "repenting and being converted." Paul speaks of it in Romans as "being alive from the dead."

Second Corinthians 5:17, says: "If any man be in Christ, he is a new creature, old things are passed away. Behold, old things have become new."

In Ephesians, Paul speaks of it as "quickening," or being made alive from the dead. In Colossians, Paul calls it a "putting off of the old man with his deeds and putting on the new man, which is renewed in knowledge after the image of Him that created him."

17

In Titus, he calls it "the washing of regeneration and the renewing of the Holy Spirit."

In Peter, the Apostle says, "being made partakers of the divine nature." In the Epistle of John, he calls it "passing from death unto life."

If you pick up a Church of England Catechism it reads this way: "A death unto sin and a new birth unto righteousness."

The Bible teaches it, the church teaches it: you must be converted for the forgiveness of your sins.

The Bible says, "All of us have sinned." You might not have done all the sins in the book but you are a sinner, and I am a sinner. We have all come short of the glory of God. We have all failed to meet God's moral requirements.

Everyone of us has told a lie sometime, somewhere. Everyone of us has had lust in our hearts, sometime, somewhere.

We have sinned against God, and this sin has come between us and God and this sin causes death—physical death, spiritual death, and eternal death. That means separation from God—judgment and hell.

Now the greatest thing in life is to find forgiveness of sin. We have only a few years here.

The Bible says that "our lives are spent as a tale that is told."

The Bible says that our lives pass quicker than a weaver's shuttle.

The Bible says that life is only a shadow.

The Bible says that it is like the flower: it blooms and fades.

18

Our life passes so quickly that it is soon gone. God gives us a few days, a few months, a few years, to find one thing, and that is reconciliation to Him and forgiveness. God's forgiveness is the greatest thing in life—worth more than a billion dollars. It is worth more than a business empire. It is worth more than a glamorous career. It is worth more than an education. It is worth more than *anything.*

To be forgiven of sin! God says the only way that you can be forgiven your sins and escape the judgment of hell is to be converted!

Secondly, you need to be converted for your acceptance by God. Because, you see, just as you are now, God cannot accept you. Why, with your present evil nature, if you went to heaven, it would be hell to you.

Suppose you went to heaven as you are. You don't enjoy a prayer service down here on earth, you don't even enjoy a church service, you go because it is a duty—something you have always done.

It is traditional, but you do not particularly like to go to church. You do not particularly like to be with God's people; you do not like to read the Bible; you do not like to worship God.

Why, you would be miserable in heaven because that is all they are going to do up there.

They will be worshiping God day and night and if you could not stand that for an hour down here, you would be squirming, you would surely be in hell after the first three or four hours of being in heaven.

So you don't want to go to heaven with your present nature. You see, with your present nature, not changed by the power of Christ, you would be out of place up there.

Now you are a sinner, you have offended God. The Bible speaks of us as enemies of God. We have broken the laws of God. We deserve judgment and we are going to get judgment.

Somebody said, "But all I'm asking for is justice." No, I am not asking for justice, because if I were to get justice, I would be lost. I am not asking for justice. I want God's mercy.

And I see it in Jesus Christ's death on the Cross, when He shed His blood for my sins. I see in His death the love of God, the mercy of God, the grace of God extended toward me. And when I come and, by faith, receive His Son, I am said to be converted and changed and God comes into my life.

A new life begins. I have become a partaker of the Divine Nature and in that moment, I am said to be justified —just as if I had never sinned.

In other words, God does not only forgive us, God places us in a position higher than Adam before he sinned. We are placed in God's sight as though we had never committed a sin, so that God even forgets our sin.

We need to be converted for entrance into Heaven. Jesus said, "except ye be converted and become as little children, ye shall not enter into the kingdom of heaven."

I did not say it; Jesus said it. Do you think Jesus was lying? You haven't been converted? Then you will not get to heaven. That is what Jesus said.

You say, "Oh, we will make it somehow, for God is a wonderful God. He is a God of love and He is a God of mercy. Certainly He is going to get us there."

Yes, He is a God of mercy, He is a God of love, not

willing that any should perish but that all should come to repentance.

But if you go on rejecting Christ and go on without conversion to Him, there is nothing God can do about it, because you sin away the mercy and the grace of God and there remains nothing but judgment to come.

God is not only mercy, not only love and grace; God is judgment. And the wrath of God shall be poured out upon men who are outside of Christ. Would you enter heaven today? Suppose you dropped dead right where you are, would you enter the Kingdom of Heaven? Are you sure? How many of you know that you will be alive tomorrow? Are you willing to gamble the next twenty-four hours, to gamble on the fact that you will live?

I believe everyone is counting on being in heaven. You are counting on being saved. You are counting on being received by God into heaven. Yet, you have not even done what God said are the basic requirements of entrance into the Kingdom.

Jesus said, no one will enter the Kingdom who has not been converted.

You say, "Well, Billy, what is involved in conversion? What is conversion?" Well, first there must be repentance. What does repentance mean?

Repentance means to change your mind, to change your feelings, to change your purpose, to change your conduct.

It is intellectual, it is emotional, it is volitional.

It means that I look at my sins and I'm willing to say to God, "I am a sinner."

I talked to a man one day and before I could get

21

a word in edgewise he was telling me how good he was, how much he had given away, what he was doing for other people.

All of that is fine but that does not merit your salvation.

The Bible says that all our righteousness is as filthy rags in the sight of God.

You can obey the Golden Rule and still not be in the Kingdom of God.

Nicodemus was as fine a Pharisee as ever lived. He kept the law, but Jesus said, "Nicodemus, you need to be born again."

A rich young ruler had kept all the commandments, but Jesus said, "If you want to enter heaven, one thing you lack, you must admit that you are not fully committed to God. Your love of money stands in the way."

Are you willing to admit that?

Intellectually you must say, "I am a sinner."

Recognize you are a sinner, and if you ever get a vision of God, who He is, and what He is, you will in all humility, say, "O God, *I* am a sinner."

Do you know how God compares you?

He does not compare you with other people. You may be better than 90 percent of the people in America.

God compares you to Jesus. He compares you with His Son. And there is not a person here who can stand up and say, "I'm as good as Jesus."

If you come short of Jesus, you are a sinner. You must recognize that. You must acknowledge it, and then there is a change of feeling.

You know, it's a strange thing today that people don't want any emotion in religion. I never tell a death-bed story. I never tell a story to try to work on people emotionally. I think that is wrong.

I think that it is deceitful on the part of the evangelist or the preacher to work deliberately on the emotions of people. Having said that, I agree with Dr. W. E. Sangster, the great Methodist preacher of London.

Dr. Sangster said some time ago, "Anybody that will go to a football game and shout, and anybody that will go to a baseball game and yell 'kill the umpire,' and then say you should never have any emotion in religion, that man does not deserve any attention whatsoever."

Isn't it a strange thing that we can sit in front of a television set and bite our fingernails off watching "Bonanza," or when the baseball game is on we watch the World Series with all our emotions running wild, and in the background people are shouting.

But in church, if you shed a tear, or even smile or have any emotion or any feeling, you are suspect immediately.

No wonder Dr. John MacKay, the former president of Princeton Theological Seminary, speaking to the students on the opening day of school a few years ago, said, "Nazism had fire, Communism has fire and *the Church must catch fire!*"

We need some fire in our churches today. I don't mean shouting. I don't even mean yelling "amen." I mean that expectancy, that enthusiasm, that urgency, that fervor, which the early church had.

They had seen a risen Savior. They went out to tell the world about it.

Every night we see people coming here, shedding a few tears. Thank God for tears. We have too few tears over

23

sin today, although we have tears about everything else. The Bible says "Godly sorrow worketh repentance."

There is a change of purpose involved in repentance. It means that you are willing to turn from sin. You may not have power to turn from your sins. Some may have battles with habits of sin even after conversion. I have seen it time after time. But there must be a willingness in the weakest heart to turn from sin.

You must be willing. God does not say you have to turn; He says you must be willing and, if you are willing, He will help you to turn.

Then there must be a change of conduct. Old things must pass away and behold, all things must become new.

Jesus said, "By their fruits ye shall know them." If I see a man who is going on living habitually in sin, I know that man has never been converted.

He does not have a new nature. He may look like a Christian at times. You can take a pig, give him a bath, put a ribbon on him, dress him up, put a little Chanel No. 5 on him, polish his hoofs a little bit, take him in the living room and put him in a chair. He looks like a wonderful, clean pig.

You say, "Why, this pig is changed. This is a different pig." You open the door and then see what happens. The nature of the pig has never been changed and the pig runs right to the mud puddle. That is where he belongs.

Now take some of you people on Sunday morning. You dress up and put a little halo on your head, and you go to church and sit down and look like a saint.

Everybody says, "Isn't he a fine, upstanding citizen." While you are watching the preacher, you are thinking about "Gunsmoke" the night before.

You reach in your pocket and you pull out a fifty-cent piece. You flip it into the basket, as though you were giving God a tip.

You say, "Lord, here you are; here is your tip for the week."

You get out of church, shake hands with the minister, go home, take the halo off, take your wings off, pick up your pitchfork and the horns begin to grow again. No change has taken place.

But any change that God makes in your life is a permanent change! Old things pass away; your life is different.

A change takes place when you come to Christ, and God brings about this tremendous transformation that we call the new birth.

Secondly, not only is repentance needed but faith —and this word faith means more than just belief.

I hear a lot of people who go around and say, "Believe in the Lord Jesus Christ and thou shall be saved."

That's true, but you don't know what the word "believe" means. The word "believe" just doesn't get over to us in English. That word "believe" means more than just intellectual faith, because the Bible says, "The devil believes."

Why, the Devil is a fundamentalist, and he is orthodox. He believes in Christ. He believes in the Bible. He believes the whole business of religion. He is even in the religion business.

Intellectually, he believes in the dogma, he believes in the creed. But the Devil has never been saved and he is not going to Heaven. On Sunday morning many of you can recite the Apostles' Creed through without making a mistake.

But I tell you that is not enough. There must be a real commitment to Christ. There must be a complete surrender to Christ.

Have you done that? Have you come with everything you have and allowed Him to change your life in full surrender?

Can you say, "Jesus is my Savior. I am trusting in Him and Him alone for salvation. I am not trusting in anything or anybody but Christ. By faith I surrender to Him. I am willing to obey Him and follow Him from this moment on."

Now, you have head belief and heart belief, but your will must also be involved.

You must be willing to say, "I *will* receive Christ." Christ appeals to the will of men. Jesus said, "Ye will not come to Me that ye might have life." Jesus didn't say, you couldn't come. He said, "Ye *will* not come."

You will not come. There are hundreds of you that ought to come and give your life to Christ. But Jesus says, "Ye will not come." You are not willing for your will to be surrendered to the will of Christ.

Jesus said, "If ye are not willing to confess Me before men, I will not confess you before my Father, which is in Heaven." You will not. You put up a barrier.

Your will does not bend to Him. "If any man *will* come after Me," said Jesus. Now the moment that you come to Christ by repentance and by faith, God in a miraculous and glorious way changes your life.

He forgives all the past. He gives you a new nature.

He gives you new values and new motives and a new direction for your life. He puts a smile on your face and a spring in your step and a joy in your soul.

Now, He does not remove your problems. In fact, I think after you come to Christ, you may face more problems. But in the midst of your problems there will be peace and grace and strength and a new dimension for living.

Have you been converted? Are you sure of it? If you are not certain, I ask you to come. In the late eighteenth century, William Wilberforce was converted and almost singlehandedly broke the shackles of slavery in England.

On November 29, 1785, he was converted, and he wrote in his diary these words: "I am wretched, miserable, blind and naked. What infinite love that Christ should die to save such a sinner as me."

And that night Wilberforce, only twenty-three years of age, gave his life to Christ and changed the whole course of history.

How many of you know the origin of the Y.M.C.A.? Who founded it? In the latter part of the nineteenth century George Williams was converted in England's west country.

He later wrote how he knelt down at the back of an empty shop. "I cannot describe to you the joy and peace which flowed into my soul when first I saw that the Lord Jesus had died for my sins and that they were all forgiven."

I tell you, when you come to Christ—I do not care when it is, I do not care where it is, or how it is—when you come, you will have to come by repentance and faith, trusting in Him and His death and Resurrection alone for salvation.

If you haven't come, if you haven't met Christ, I am asking you to do it now.

You may be a member of the church. But you are not sure that you have actually met Christ and been converted.

You want to be sure and you want to settle it. Do it now!

An invitation to go forward

IT MAY BEGIN WITH A SWIFT SURREN-
DER. IT MAY BE A GRADUAL GROWTH.
BUT THE COUNSELING ROOM IS
WHERE THE CHIPS GO DOWN, WHERE
CARE OF THE SOUL BEGINS.

"Eye hath not seen, nor ear
heard, neither have en-
tered into the heart of man,
the things which God hath
prepared for them that
love him."

I CORINTHIANS 2:9

We come now to the great mystery.

The moment has no name, but it will be remembered—if it comes—as long as life itself.

It is initiated by compounding factors, by pressures from within a person and from without, but when all is said and done, the ultimate result is the work of the Holy Spirit.

Within, the heart may ache and tug, beset by memories of sins committed and good deeds omitted. A self-searching, inward-looking something is stalking the corridors of the mind. Locked rooms are bursting open and ancient ghosts parading. Although among many of those hearing an evangelist's invitation, no movement may be seen, no upheaval suspected, nevertheless deep currents are surely moving, beating, swirling.

The evangelist's voice suddenly lowers, and the audience leans forward to catch every word.

His plea may be soft spoken but it is packed suddenly with an electric urgency. The words vary only a little from night to night and from city to city. In New York's Madison Square Garden, over a decade ago, Billy Graham said:

"Don't let distance keep you from Christ. It's a long way but Christ went all the way to the Cross because He loved you. Certainly you can come these few steps and give your life to Him. I am going to ask that every head be bowed right now in prayer."

The choir began to sing, "Just As I Am," and Graham continued: "Come right now while the choir sings. The decision is up to you. No one can make it for you. I remember when I sat there in that tabernacle in Charlotte, North Carolina, they were singing the last verse of the song when I went forward. That first step was the hardest I ever took in my life. But when I took it God did the rest. I woke up the next morning and I *knew* I had been changed. You can make a great decision tonight that will change your life. You can be born again and you'll never be the same . . ."

Preaching in Denver ten years later, he said:

"Give yourselves to Christ tonight. Let Him forgive your sins. Let Him come into your heart and change your life. I'm going to ask you to get up out of your seats, hundreds of you, get up out of your seats right now and come and stand on this field.

"You say, 'But why do I have to get up and come?' Every person Jesus called in the New Testament was called publicly. There's something about coming forward and standing here. It's an outward expression of an inward decision.

"I'm asking you tonight to say yes to Christ. To say, 'I want Him to be my Lord and Master.' Just get up and come right now. You may be in the choir, you may be a Sunday-school teacher, you may be a parent and you need Christ to help you make the right kind of home. We're going to wait on you. Quickly, that's it, quickly, come from everywhere. People are already coming. You get up and join them. Get up and come and receive Jesus Christ . . ."

This invitation is never a "Come one, come all" summons designed merely to wring every possible sinner from the audience. Graham once wrote, "I have made the invitation hard and difficult, and as clear as I believe it can possibly be made, yet they come. There seems to be no letup in the stream of humanity coming to Christ." All around the world, the people come. At Wembley Stadium in England, on a rainy Saturday in May of 1956, over 100,000 persons listened to the invitation. A newspaperman described their response:

> There was no emotional hysteria; only a very deep reverence as hundreds upon hundreds moved down onto the emerald green carpet of Wembley turf while the choir sang 'Just As I Am.' Down they came in drizzling rain. Men of all classes. Husbands, wives, children. Whole families came forward together, hand in hand. Within a few moments the rapidly moving stream had flooded Wembley's famous turf with one colorful mass of humanity.

And still many persons high in the terraces could not get to the arena because of barriers. Graham saw them and said, "You can accept Jesus Christ where you are. Just wave your handkerchief as a confession that you have ac-

33

cepted him into your lives." At once, hundreds of handkerchiefs fluttered.

George Burnham describes a meeting in Paris in
his book *Billy Graham, A Mission Accomplished.*

Now he was in the process of giving an invitation for
people to renounce their sin and turn by faith to Jesus
Christ. But four persons didn't give him time to finish.
They arose from their seats in different sections of the
Vélodrome and walked to the platform before the appeal
was given.

The first was a middle-aged Frenchman. He walked
with shoulders erect and head held high as if he had
waited all his life to find peace with God and couldn't
wait any longer. A woman joined him. Two men left
their seats. Streams of people poured forward . . . a boy
with a crew cut, followed by a sophisticated woman. A
woman in a wheel chair pushed by a friend . . . two
French soldiers, a man humped with age, a girl in pigtails,
a mother with twin daughters, a young beauty with a
French hairdo. Nothing like this had ever happened before in Paris.

After a service in Palamcottah, India, Graham
wrote in his diary: "I preached for about an hour and had
tremendous power and liberty. I knew that the message of
God was going home. When we closed, I gave the invitation and Pentecost fell. People began to run forward and
fall upon their knees. Some of them began to scream to
God for mercy; others were saying, 'Jesus, save me! Jesus,
save me!' until about 3,000 or 4,000 people had come, and
we had to stop the invitation for there was no room for
anyone else."

34

Around the world in New Zealand, Warner Hutchinson wrote in *Let The People Rejoice:*

High up in a dark stand, one decided for Christ. The platform was so far away that facial features of Billy Graham were indistinct. There was no chance to be moved by the penetrating look of his eyes. Only his voice was heard. The one, so far away, realized the decision was his, and his alone. Others from behind him were slowly walking down the steps to the grass. He was hardly aware of them for he was struggling so within. Then he decided —Christ is for me. And he joined 3,000 others on the grass. But for him it was no mass movement. It was the most highly individualistic thing he had ever done. Indeed, he had now become a whole person.

A Chicago woman wrote, "I hung onto my seat with might and main, but I felt myself lifted and suddenly I was out in the aisle walking forward on feet that seemed to wear wings."

A California divorcee wrote, "I knew on the instant that my surrender was complete and I couldn't get to the front fast enough. I was cleansed and full of joy for the first time in years."

A Georgia businessman reported, "I felt uncomfortable and angry, so I left the building. I was already out on the sidewalk when I suddenly turned around and headed straight for the front. Nobody can tell me that I did that of my own free will."

A young Australian matron said: "I had a big, broad grin on my face when the appeal was made to go forward at the Sydney Showground on Mother's Day afternoon, 1959. It was the last meeting of the crusade, and, incidentally, the only one my husband and I attended.

"I was absolutely disinterested in anything spiritual; I had never been to Sunday school. I only went to the crusade because everybody else seemed to be making their way there too, and one has to do what everybody else does! I believed that 'somebody' must have made this world and all that is in it, but my attitude toward God and Christianity in general was one of complete apathy.

"My husband had risen first under conviction at the invitation, but not I. I remember that Billy Graham was speaking of 'a straight and narrow way,' which did not interest me; but when he threw out the challenge that there were those who were seeking for something, they knew not what, and were living lives that could never be satisfied—then I began to listen more earnestly! This was *me* he was talking about!

"I found myself standing in front of the platform that Sunday afternoon in the rain. 'I'm a sinner,' I said. As I said this the Holy Spirit hit me.

"We had lived in Malaya for years, and our life had been one of drinking, smoking, parties, sordid talk—self-indulgence in every way!

"From the moment we walked out of the Showground He has kept us both from the temptation of drink and the life it entailed. We gave up nothing ourselves. The Lord himself has taken away our liking for the things that would weaken us."

Billy Graham says, "I find that people want to make a definite commitment to Christ. The New Testament bears this out. Jesus gave many invitations. Zacchaeus had to come down out of a tree to make his commitment of faith. The Philippian jailor, who knew only the Gospel that he had heard Paul and Silas singing in his prison, was converted that very same night in the midst of an earthquake. You could have said, 'That decision won't last.' But a church was established in Philippi."

Wherever he is, if a man goes forward, either in fact or in spirit, the result is a change.

What takes place? Psychologists, psychiatrists, theologians and evangelists have all tried to explain.

Gordon Allport, noted psychologist, says: "A man's religion is the audacious bid he makes to bind himself to creation and the Creator. It is his ultimate attempt to enlarge and complete his personality by finding the supreme context in which he rightly belongs."

Then perhaps conversion is the ultimate spiritual step toward that end.

Graham has said, "I believe that before a person comes to Christ the Holy Spirit convicts him of sin. This brings about misery. And this misery brings about pressure on his will to do something about it. I feel that people in our meetings go through a terrible spiritual struggle about, 'Will I give in to Christ or not? Will I make Him the spiritual sovereign of my life?' And this takes the form of the Holy Spirit speaking to him and disturbing him.

"When the rich young ruler rejected Christ, the Bible says he went away grieved. You can write a lot of psychological language into that word 'grieved.' He was disturbed; he was not happy about it, and when the Holy Spirit is dealing with our sin, we feel miserable."

But explanations seem only to deepen the mystery. Is there another approach? Could we learn more by inquiring: what does conversion do to a person?

It regenerates men, this is beyond dispute. In *Twice-born Men,* author Harold Begbie gives many dramatic illustrations and then makes the striking assertion: "Conversion is the only means by which a radically bad person can be changed into a radically good person."

Conversion creates a *new* person. We have an abundance of Scriptural evidence here, as well as many psychological insights. Dr. Robert O. Ferm, in *The Psychology of Christian Conversion,* says:

> In religious awakening or conversion, whether it comes gradually or suddenly, the whole self comes under the power of a new master sentiment. Because it creates a new organization of the entire person, it brings about a new birth indeed . . . This new creature, it should be remembered, has within him many of the old qualities and characteristics. In other words, his identity with his preconversion self is recognizable. Yet he is different. A new organization integrates his personality, an organization which has never before existed. The individual may, therefore, very appropriately be called a new creature.

Conversion will change a man and it will make him into a new person, but this is not the end. Once a sinner surrenders his pride and responds to the evangelist's invitation, he stands in desperate need of nourishment and assistance. Some evangelists wage a victorious campaign right up through the personal crisis, and then stop. An inquirer might walk to the front, receive a hurried handshake from the preacher, and promptly be forgotten. Critics who charged that itinerant evangelists were more interested in swollen boxscores than in saving souls were often correct.

But when a new convert—Graham calls him an inquirer—goes forward at a Billy Graham crusade, no matter how many others are taking the identical step at the same time, he becomes an individual with a unique problem to be met and solved personally. The painstaking concern with which Graham and his team go about this task of nurture is one of the features that sets his ministry apart. It is also safe to say that only a small minority of churches trouble themselves to provide an equal amount of guidance for their own "newborn."

So young Jane Doe, who has come to a crusade service in her hometown stadium, sits now in the bleachers with a group of friends. Within her heart, she is torn and worried as the evangelist reveals to her consciousness the extent of her sin. She hears his voice, hears his words of invitation, and suddenly she accepts their meaning. Rising, she moves into the aisle and begins the long march forward to the altar.

Other men, women, and children are all about her, some with dry eyes and some with tears on their cheeks, and presently another woman of Jane's approximate age is walking at her side, carrying a Bible and wearing the badge of a counselor. If Jane had been a teenager, a coed might have risen softly to accompany her. If she had been a man, another male would come. So the growing assemblage before the pulpit is never a solid mass of emotional novices, as some have thought, but consists instead of careful pairings, pupil to teacher, inquirer to counselor, each of whom will soon undertake the very private business of spiritual nourishment.

The counselor, whose prototype was usually an untrained "personal worker" in the campaigns of the last century, is now a carefully coached consultant and Bible student. Charles Riggs, in charge of training counselors for many major crusades, says, "One of the counselor's first obligations is to give deeply of himself. He becomes a spiritual parent sharing his knowledge with his child. The second chapter of Thessalonians describes the ideal attitude, saying, 'Being affectionately desirous of you, we were willing to have imparted unto you not only the Gospel of God, but also our own souls, because ye were dear to us.' "

Pastors of cooperating churches appoint these counselors. Prior to a crusade, thousands of them may meet for study in the evening, usually twice a week, for months.

Each night, they await the end of Billy Graham's message, anticipating the harvest. Occasionally he must overcome physical illness. "Preached on 'The End of the World,' using the story of Noah," he once wrote in his diary. "Had great liberty and did not feel bound by my hoarse throat. They started streaming forward before I was even through the invitation. I am sure that something like a thousand came forward tonight. It was by far the greatest response we have yet seen. Certainly God is moving mightily. The promise of the Lord rings in my ears as I go to bed. 'Fear not, nor be dismayed; tomorrow go out against them, for the Lord will be with you.' "

The evangelist leans forward to greet the inquirers. His voice is tired and solemn as he says that they will not be kept long but that several matters require a brief discussion. And then he leads them all in a unique prayer of confession and repentance, pausing after each phrase to allow them to repeat his simple but explicit words.

"Dear God," he says. (Dear God, Jane repeats.)

"I come to you as a sinner." (The inquirers echo each line clearly.)

"I am sorry for my sins."

"I believe that Christ died for my sins."

"Right now, I trust and receive Him as my own personal Savior, and acknowledge Him as my Master."

"Be merciful to me a sinner, and save me now."

"Give me victory over all my doubts and temptations."

"Help me to live for You in the fellowship of the Church."

"And now, thank you, Lord, for forgiving and saving me."

"In Jesus' name, Amen."

Probably this is the first prayer Jane has said aloud since she was a child. Her Rubicon has been crossed. As she ventures a smile, she notices that others, both men and women, seem to be standing straighter.

In earlier and smaller crusades, this prayer was made within the walls of an adjacent inquiry room, but as crowds of converts grew larger, it became Graham's custom to lead it himself and to end the counseling session in the open. And an unexpected blessing accrued. Walter Smythe, Graham's director of crusades, says, "We found that many persons in the audience who had not come forward were repeating it along with the others, pledging their lives to Christ. Later, many of them would write and tell us that they had joined some church."

After the prayer, if the service is in a stadium, the counseling begins at once. If the service is in an auditorium, the crowd will usually be directed to an adjacent room. In some cities, a tent has been used. In New York,

41

the stables of Madison Square Garden, occupied annually by circus animals and show horses, were hung with bunting and served well enough.

Within this hall, rows of folding chairs face a central platform. Every other chair holds an envelope of literature for the use of the counselors. As Jane Doe enters, she and her partner are directed to a seat by an older person, usually a minister who wears a badge saying "Advisor." A member of the team, or perhaps Billy Graham himself, calls the group to order and explains the significance of their presence.

Soon, the preliminaries are over and the mass dissolves into hundreds of unique pairs, each seeking the same goal in its own way. And here lies much of the genius of Graham's evangelism. From this moment on, the counselors that his team has trained become all important, each probing as expertly as he knows how for the inquirer's deepest need. Charles Riggs says, "Each person who comes forward brings along a different problem. People vary. The relationship between the counselor and the seeker cannot be cut and dried, with a card-index answer to every woe. Tonight's experience must not provide a memory of a mass of humanity stumbling forward but rather a moment when the inquirer strides victoriously into the light."

In his view, evangelism is a four-ply assignment to God's people.

First, present the facts to the inquirer, which is the responsibility of the evangelist.

Second, offer him an invitation to accept Christ.

Third, lead him through the prayer of commitment.

Fourth, review his understanding of his commitment, seeing that all the pieces fit together, and rearranging them if need be.

A doctor may have many patients in a waiting room, Riggs explains, but he cannot call them all into his consulting room at the same time and arrive at a diagnosis of what is wrong with each one. He must take them singly, individually, and this is why Billy Graham augments himself with thousands of trained counselors. Each must face his own "patient" with love and insight.

He must ask and find out, for example, if the inquirer has called on the Lord. "For whosoever shall call upon the name of the Lord shall be saved," the Bible says. Riggs, who counsels nightly during a crusade says he never forgets to ask: "Have you called on the Lord?"

Most inquirers come forward to seek salvation. Others come for assurance that they have not strayed, some for restoration to the faith, and a surprising number to dedicate their lives to God's service. But the majority are seekers for the way to enter God's Kingdom, and Riggs and his counselors must first determine their awareness of their sin.

"Do you understand that you are a sinner?" they ask.

If the reply is in the affirmative, they continue: "And why did Jesus Christ come into the world?"

"To save sinners," the seeker usually says.

"What did He do to save sinners?"

"He died on the Cross and took our sins on himself."

"Well, if He died for us, does that mean that everyone on earth is automatically saved?"

"No, not everyone."

"Then what must you do to be saved?"

There is only one answer. In his sermon, just concluded, Billy Graham explained it carefully, step by step. Sooner or later, the inquirer puts his understanding into words, boiling the issue down to his personal commitment to Jesus.

"Have you committed yourself to Jesus?" Riggs asks.

And the inquirer stands at bay, quietly and lovingly stripped of all hindrance to his understanding surrender.

If a person is not quite certain of his dedication, Riggs may say, "You've come forward to receive Christ. How do you know this is what you must do?"

"Well, it says so in the Bible."

"Then God is saying it, isn't He?"

"Yes, I guess He is."

"And there's no higher authority than God, is there?"

"No, of course not."

"Then you accept the Word of God, don't you?"

Again, the inquirer is at bay, he can accept or reject, but the decision he makes for or against Jesus is now clear cut and precise.

When it is in the affirmative, as is generally the case, Riggs puts it all in a capsule for the novice. "Think of it like this," he says. "God says it. On faith, you believe it. And that settles it."

Dan Piatt, another Graham deputy with vast experience in counseling and follow-up training, says, "We believe three things are involved in every inquirer: his emotions, intellect, and will. In the emotions, we are

44

moved by the facts. A person will say, 'I ought to believe.' The intellect, in studying facts, says, 'Yes, they are reasonable.' But the will which is the hardest to move must finally say, 'I will receive Christ.' ''

In his counselor training schools, Piatt often makes his point with this analogy: "Take a man who is madly in love. He may have a great emotional stirring, but he is not married. He may come to the point of giving intellectual assent, saying, 'Honey, this makes sense. We ought to get married,' but still he is not married. Not until he stands before witnesses, bends his will to hers, and says, 'I do!'—only at that moment, and not before, is that man married.

"So it is with conversion. We may have a great emotional stirring after we have heard the facts that Jesus died for us and is willing to forgive our sins, but that still does not mean we have been born into the family of God."

So the counselor who is sitting with Jane Doe asks her friendly, probing questions to make certain that she is genuinely committing herself to Christ, and when the answer is clear the moment is sealed with a short prayer.

All around the room—or the playing field—hundreds of other couples are in close communion, some on their knees, some reading softly from Bibles, talking, writing. Their voices make a gentle din. Jane's counselor offers a pamphlet. "We have some literature to help you these first weeks. We want you to understand everything you are doing. Here's a paragraph called 'My Commitment.' It might help for you to read it aloud."

Jane reads quietly, like others about her. "Confessing that I am a sinner, and believing that Jesus Christ died for me, by God's grace I now turn from sin and receive Christ as my own personal Savior. I acknowledge Him as my Lord and Master, and by His help, I now dedicate myself to serve Him in the fellowship of the church and will seek daily to do His will in all areas of my life."

"That's a big order, isn't it?" the counselor says.

"It sure is."

"Is it too big for you?"

"Oh, no."

She hands Jane a pen. "There's a place for you to sign it, with the date. In a way, this is your new birth certificate."

This interview may lead an inquirer through eight separate steps to full personal commitment. The counselor says, "There's a plan of salvation for all of us, Jane. Do you know what the Bible tells about it?"

Jane says, "I'd rather you would tell me."

"It begins with rebellious, sinful man," the counselor says. "Because man is sinful and separate from God, he cannot hope to have eternal life. But God so loved the world, you remember, that He sent His only Son. Why did He send Jesus? He did it because He wanted to reconcile men to himself, to give them the most precious treasure in existence, which is eternal life in God's Kingdom. But He was unable to do this because men were full of sin.

"So He sent His Son, Jesus Christ, to pay the penalty in behalf of mankind. Yes, God sent Jesus to die, to be sacrificed on the Cross in order that *you* might be cleansed of your sins. When Jesus died, he took all your sins onto His own shoulders back there in Jerusalem. And thereby, He made you, Jane Doe, eligible for the treasure of salvation. But first, something else had to happen. Do you know what that was?"

Jane's eyes are shining but she shakes her head.

"Now, man was without sin, but he was also still without God," the counselor says. "So God offered man His own eternal forgiveness and fatherhood—the Bible calls it grace—on one condition. He said, 'Believe by faith that Jesus Christ is My Son, that He died for you, that He rose on the third day, and that He is become your Lord and Master. Do all that, God said to man, and then you will have salvation and eternal life in the Kingdom.' "

Jane blinks, saying "I've never understood it quite like that before."

The counselor opens her Bible and settles down. Obviously, this matter of understanding one's commitment is not to be rushed. Jane begins to relax, and to listen with greater care.

"Few people have any idea of how plainly God speaks in the Scriptures," the counselor says. "We've made up a little Bible Study Course that clears up many things. Let's go through Lesson One right now."

Jane accepts the book opened before her and reads the first question: "What does God say about the fact of sin?"

"The answer is right here," the counselor says pointing to a verse in her Bible. "Here! Why don't you read it aloud, and then write it down in the lesson folder. That way, you'll never forget it."

Jane reads and then writes, "For all have sinned, and come short of the glory of God."

On rare occasions, the counselor will lead through each and every step; more often, after the inquirer's needs are understood, only certain of those steps will be pertinent. But one paragraph that is rarely omitted reads: "For God so loved blank that He gave His only begotten Son, that if blank believes in Him, blank should not perish. . . ."

The counselor tells Jane, "Write your own name in those blank spaces."

She writes, "For God so loved Jane, that He gave His only begotten Son, that if Jane believes in Him, Jane should not perish but Jane would have everlasting life."

She sinks back, eyes closed, pressing her hands together as if to contain the wonder. "Oh, how can I ever live up to all this?" she asks.

The counselor opens her Bible to I Corinthians, 10:13. "The Bible answers that, too." She reads: "There hath no temptation taken you but such as is common to man; but God is faithful, who will not suffer you to be tempted above that ye are able; but will, with the temptation, also make way to escape that ye may be able to bear it." The counselor is aware of the difficulty presented by the obscure phraseology of King James' scholars, and adds, "In other words, you'll be tempted, all right, but God will help you to withstand it. The Bible promises God's help, not occasionally, but always. It says clearly, 'God is faithful.' "

Among the couples, hands rise here and there above bowed heads, a signal with which a counselor summons an older advisor. While Jane waits, she reads a message Billy Graham has written to each inquirer containing suggestions for the development of spiritual maturity.

He urges daily Bible reading, daily prayers, and

daily witnessing to others. And the inquirer must affiliate with a church as soon as possible.

Now, a modicum of bookkeeping must be done, writing down the inquirer's preferred denomination and church, business, age, et cetera. Quite often, telephone numbers are exchanged.

And then the advisor arrives. He wears an inconspicuous badge and is almost always a local pastor or prominent layman. If difficulties in understanding the Scriptures have arisen, he will try to straighten them out. Usually, he needs only to confirm an inquirer's commitment by asking questions which elicit the exactness of repentance, surrender and faith.

"The process of putting one's new thoughts and feelings into words," Riggs says, "is usually a convert's first opportunity to testify publicly of his surrender to Christ. And this is most important. We can explain and talk till we are black in the face, but until we help the new-born to begin his Christian life—to *do* something— we have accomplished nothing."

So Jane Doe is prepared to return to her friends and family, and to confront them as a new person, as a newborn Christian, with a singing heart but with feet on the ground. The advisor's hand grips hers warmly. "Good night," he says. "And may the Lord keep and bless you always."

Jane makes her way back to the seats where her companions wait, becoming more aware with every step that her spirit is overflowing with the sudden, blinding rightness of things.

Within forty-eight hours, she will receive a phone

call or a letter from her counselor. The minister of the church she has elected to attend, or a layman, will come to visit her in her home. Presently, another Bible lesson will come in the mail from Graham's Minneapolis headquarters. And this is the beginning of the follow-up, the thoughtful process which nourishes and shepherds until the new wisdom and strength reach their full Christian growth.

Many newspapers have made spot checks a month after a successful crusade and concluded that not much has changed after all. Billy Graham says they should wait. Their investigation is too much like a reporter counting all the newborn babies in a city for one month and then, in the next week, announcing that they have made no impact on their city. But wait until those babies mature. Wait until they take over businesses and schools and city hall. Then, and only then, is the time right to measure their impact.

Surely, God's babies are not so different. Christian maturity is a gradual process taking from a few months to many years. Jane Doe is now a child of God, but her maturation must evolve out of trials and temptations, defeats and victories. Whatever happens, never again will she feel deserted, helpless, or useless, for the Bible says, "God is faithful. . . ."

Even when all that happened to Jane is known, you still have not penetrated the mystery. You are still an outsider unless you also joined her in that long march forward, unless you too accepted God's grace, and the conditions thereof.

To the intellect of most men, the new birth that comes, when it comes, is as much of an enigma as the descent of the Holy Spirit on the human soul. But that it is real and that man is changed is the testimony of thousands.

Nor is the experience limited to novices who are making their professions of faith for the first time. By the thousands, as letters and interviews attest, men and women who have labored long in the church, even those who have preached and counseled, receive the same extraordinary blessing, to their immeasurable benefit and joy.

Billy Graham once looked down into the faces of those who had come forward and was astonished to recognize an elderly acquaintance. This was a distinguished pastor and theology professor, as well as a famous author of religious books. Yet he stood there quietly among the penitents. "Afterwards, we went up to my room and talked," Graham says. "I asked him, 'Why did you come forward tonight?' His reply was, 'All these years that I have preached and written, I have never once had peace or the assurance that I had been born again. The older I grew, the worse it felt, and the more frightened I became. Tonight, I had peace for the first time in my life.' "

To some inquirers making the "audacious attempt" to relate their lives to God's Kingdom, the new birth provides a reality beyond compare.

"When it came to me, I could not explain what had happened," Samuel Chadwick describes it, "but I was aware of things unspeakable and full of glory. Some results were immediate. There came into my soul a deep peace, a thrilling joy, and a new sense of power. My mind was quickened. I felt that I had received a new faculty of understanding. There was a new sense of spring and vitality, a new power of endurance and a strong man's exhilaration in big things. Things began to happen. What I had failed to do by strenuous endeavor, came to pass without labor. It was as when the Lord Jesus stepped into the boat that, with all the disciples rowing, had made no progress, and 'immediately the ship was at land whither they went.' It was gloriously wonderful."

And this, to a greater or lesser degree, is a portion of the treasure that comes to every John and Jane Doe.

Part Two

Their
lives

Some men build empires or bend the course of history, but greatness also lies in victory over self and pride, as these newborn lives attest.

How high a dream

AHEAD LAY ROMANCE AND SERVICE,
BUT JIM PERCY HAD NO IDEA OF SUCH
THINGS THE NIGHT THE HAND OF
JESUS TOUCHED HIM IN HIS SLEEP.

It was a dream, yet it was not a dream. No dream could be so real, with the glowing figure of Jesus Christ standing there in 22-year-old Jim Percy's bedroom in New York City. Filled with astonishment, the former Mexico University student found himself trembling. Wild memories of his reckless college life assailed him, and Jim felt a sudden fear.

Swiftly, almost instantly, he knew what he must do. He flung himself down before the resplendent figure, poising on his knees in the familiar way of his boyhood in the Catholic church. His lips began to move. He was startled to hear what his lips were saying. Not the words he had been taught, not his portion of any litany, nor even an Ave Maria or Gloria Patri. Instead, he heard this plea:

"I'm sorry. . . . I'm sorry. . . . I'm sorry." Later,

he said, "I repeated it over and over and over until my heart was empty."

Then Jesus took a step toward him. Jim was still asleep but somehow he understood that this was more than a dream. The implication stunned him. He could not know it then, for he had never read his Bible, but one day he would compare his vision with that of Isaiah.

Isaiah saw the Lord sitting on a throne, accompanied by seraphims who cried, "Holy, holy, holy. . . ." And the foundations of all the houses shook, and the air filled with smoke, and Isaiah cried, "Woe is me! For I am lost. I am a man of unclean lips and dwell in the midst of a people of unclean lips, and I have seen the King, the Lord of hosts."

But an angel plucked a live coal from the altar and touched the Prophet's mouth, and he said, "Your guilt is taken away. Your sin is forgiven."

Then the Lord's voice asked, "Whom shall I send?"

Isaiah did not know what mission was meant, what journey was promised, but the answer leaped to his lips: "Here I am! Send me."

Dreaming Jim Percy, his lips quivering with "I'm sorry. . . . I'm sorry," suddenly felt the touch of the Lord's hand, and heard his voice. It was like no other voice, with a quality that thrilled and reassured. It was not loud, yet it could have been heard for a thousand miles.

Jesus told Jim, "It's all right!"

"Never can I forget the indescribable ecstasy of the moment," he remembers.

Next morning, a troubled Jim Percy sat on the side of his bed, trying to decipher the meaning of that encounter. At his job, where he was a clerk in the export department of a plumbing house, he could not shake off the reality of his dream. Looking back over his life, he felt ashamed and humiliated, because he knew he was not the man he wanted to be. Friends noted his preoccupation, and so did his parents.

One day, passing a bookstore, he thought he heard a voice. "Buy a Bible," it called. He turned into the doorway in obedience. He bought a Bible and began to read. "I'm going to go through it from cover to cover," he promised himself.

He failed, of course. The Bible is not meant to be read in that manner. Nobody told him he should start with the New Testament, preferably with the Book of John. So he worked his way through Genesis and Exodus, wondering how those lessons of slavery and wanderings applied to life in glittering, dynamic Manhattan. Confused and angry, he finally threw the Bible aside.

"So you had a crazy dream. Forget it," his common sense told him.

"It was a message," his conscience replied.

He waited, noncommittal, like an empty sack waiting to be filled. He did not enjoy those weeks; to be empty is no fun.

"Then God began to close in on my life," he says.

The telephone rang one morning, conveying an invitation. His aunt and uncle, living on Long Island, were coming into Manhattan to attend the Billy Graham crusade.

"And what is the Billy Graham crusade?" the Catholic Percys asked. The explanation was not very satisfactory; Graham was a young evangelist who had rented

Madison Square Garden for an entire summer. Each night, he preached a simple gospel, and thousands were responding. The Percys said, "No, we don't think we'll go."

Jim went out to work without another thought, spent all that day unaware of the wings beating about his head. On the way home, a friend pressed a strip of cardboard into his hand. It was a ticket for Madison Square Garden where Graham was preaching. He blinked at the coincidence, and changed his plans.

That night, he was among the 17,000 persons who packed the Garden, watching the unfolding drama of the service, and feeling his nerves tighten with a secret message, "Jim, this is where you belong."

The friendly ushers, the selfless singing of Beverly Shea, and the massive choir with the famous star Ethel Waters in her inconspicuous place,—all these kindled a spark in the heart he had emptied during his vision.

And when Billy Graham finished his sermon, submitting his three-ply invitation, his heart caught fire. "Repent," Billy said. "I do," said Jim.

"Receive the Lord."

"I receive Him."

"Surrender yourself and follow His leading."

"I surrender, Lord."

Sitting in his seat, he recalls, "My heart responded without reservation. I knew all Mr. Graham said was right and good."

But he held himself in his seat. He thought he had surrendered, but in truth he had not. Others went forward but not Jim Percy. Graham said, "You may never have this opportunity again." Jim argued back, "Not yet! Not tonight! I want another day to think it over."

When the benediction was given and the great crowd shuffled off toward subways and taxicabs, he sat bowed and wondering for a long time, knowing the crossroads at which he stood, but incapable of movement.

Next night, he returned early, with shining, untroubled eyes. Seatmates noticed his attentiveness and then the calm confidence with which he finally arose and accepted Graham's invitation to walk down the long Garden aisle.

God's work may begin with a vision and a personal commitment, but it never ends there, as Jim Percy would soon discover. Within a few days of his going forward, a pastor had talked to him, inviting him to join his congregation. His voice was warm, his enthusiasm genuine. Delighted, Jim went to his first service, and his heart fell. The building was small and poorly furnished. His memory served up opulent images of burning candles and robed priests, of great windows warmed with stained glass in the Mexican cathedral he had visited, of a rich, traditional order of worship. "What are you doing here?" an inner voice asked. He had prayed to be guided to a good church, as his counselor at the crusade meeting had suggested. Now he sat on the hard wooden bench in a small New Jersey Gospel Church, thinking, regretting, and resisting.

The audience settled around him, smiling. Then they opened their songbooks and sang so joyously, so thrillingly, that unaccountably his heart began to pound. The sermon was as cheering as the hymns, and as forthright as the ten sermons he had heard from Billy Graham in the Garden. When it was over, warm hands thrust at him from all sides, welcoming him. He wondered if this was what Graham meant by "brothers in Christ."

59

The pastor told him, "We hope you will want to come again."

"I would like to," Jim replied, and so he united with the fellowship of believers at the Fairview Gospel Church in Fairview, New Jersey.

As the weeks passed, Jim came to feel that his rebirth in Christ meant not only that he was a new man but that he had to make a new start vocationally. His job was secure enough but it was hardly in line with what his inner mind told him was the work of the Lord. Guiding shipments of plumbing fixtures from American factories to European bathrooms was no solution to his spiritual needs.

He told his boss, "Sir, I've got to leave as soon as you can replace me."

"Got something better, Jim?" the man asked.

"I've got nothing, sir."

"Nothing! Jim, are you insane?"

"I'll find something. The Lord will guide me."

His boss wore no horns, no tail. Believing honestly that he was protecting the youth's best interests, he urged, "Stay with us awhile longer. Your friends are here. We like you. Leaving without another job is plain silly."

The mind is usually conditioned toward a search for security, and unaccustomed to the faith that believes in the literal meaning of Jesus' promises. Jim thought, "He's right. Maybe I ought to save up and then take the step." The warm hand of his boss reached his shoulder. What to do now? He wants to help me. Will I offend him if I insist on leaving? How do I know this is the right thing to do? A flashing fragment of his dream glowed for an instant and then vanished; and Jim suddenly braced himself.

60

"My mind's made up, sir."

On faith, he resigned from his steady job to accept whatever God had in mind for him. He compiled a list of religious organizations which might use his experience, and began the rounds.

The American Bible Society, the New York Bible Society, the American Tract Society, Christian missions with offices in Manhattan; one after another, he trudged from door to door to meet with disappointment. "Where next, God?" he asked, over and over.

He was well down on his list when he trudged into the modest office of the Sudan Interior Mission, in that vast acreage of decaying real estate on the west side of Manhattan's Central Park. The street was grimy and unbelievably crowded, and the brownstone front sorely needed laundering, but within he met the direct and joyous friendliness that he had found among some other Christians. Explaining his purpose, he asked if he could help.

"God opened the door," he says. "They put me to doing the same type of export work I knew so well."

Settling into his new job, he was astonished by his co-workers. None ever spoke irritably, none could bear the thought of smoking or drinking. Some even thought that attendance at Hollywood movies was disgraceful. Daily, they prayed and read their Bibles right in the office. "Puritans," he dubbed them, thinking they were the oddest ducks he had ever met, telling himself, "It's a front. They can't be for real."

Old friends called him for parties and outings. "Hello, old buddy," a voice bubbled. "We've got a wingding scheduled for Saturday. A beach party, see." He remembered other parties, and his skin began to burn. "We met some new girls," the voice urged. "You can take your pick." He turned down the invitation.

Another week, a pal from Mexico called. "We can have a quick drink together. Like old times, huh?"

He went home and prayed. He wanted with all his heart to see his pals and their pretty companions who had warmed his senses in the old days till they exploded in swift delight. Remembering those moments, the glances under long lashes, the touches, the caresses, the swelling of the ego and the mounting of pride in conquest. . . .

Suddenly, the issue was clear. An inner voice put it simply: "Make up your mind, Jim. Who is lord here? Is it your flesh or is it Jesus Christ?"

Night after night, he hurried through his dinner and into his room, shaking with the struggle inside him. "I surrendered," he cried. "Why must I feel like this now?" He locked his door and clung to his chair, sweating. He flung the key into a far corner and closed his eyes, pleading for help.

On one such night he remembered that he was not alone in his fight. God was in it, too, and awaited only the invitation presented by unquestioning faith. That night he cried, "Lord, you take over. Lord, I cannot do it, but you can."

And the tide began to turn, aided by the men and women whom he had called "Puritans," who perceived his torment and offered their love. One of them was a registered nurse and a graduate of a Canadian Bible college.

"There were times when she would sit with me until three and four in the morning counseling me and

62

praying," he recalls gratefully. "Then she would wearily head back to the city and put in a full day's work."

Before long, Jim became convinced that he wanted to live as fully as possible following the example of Jesus, and to serve others. The inspiration came not only through prayer and reading the Bible, but also from observing his new friends at the mission office. He learned that many of the persons he most admired had graduated from a small school called the Prairie Bible Institute, located across the continent in a Canadian town of 1,000 souls called Three Hills, Alberta.

Again, on faith, he resigned from his job, and made his way west. It was the autumn of 1958, slightly more than one year after the evening he had first gone to the Madison Square Garden crusade. "Coming to that Prairie campus from New York," he says, "was like stepping from the doorstep of hell into the grand entry of the New Jerusalem."

His joy was of short duration. He had never learned the art of self-discipline, nor had he formed good study habits. Poring over his books, he would pound his fists against his head in frustration, as he absorbed the great literature of the Bible, the portentous prophecies, and the theology of ancient and modern saints. For months it was torture. And then a strange calmness came to him.

He says, "As the months wore on, God in His mercy began to work in my life. His Word gradually took hold of the inner man and a new joy and victory in Christ resulted."

By springtime, he was adjusted. "What will you do this summer?" a friend asked.

"I've been wondering."

"I know a camp. Not much money, but lots of kids who need help. There's a job there. Interested?"

"I'll take it."

The summer passed quickly, divided between service and study. And he met a winsome classmate named Delia from Sutton Surrey in England. He recalls, "I was telling friends about Billy Graham's crusade in New York when one of them said, 'We have an English girl here who was converted at one of his Harringay meetings.' "

The Harringay crusade was Graham's first all-out effort in England, and antedated the New York crusade. Compared to Delia, Jim was a novice, but they found much in common.

After four years of study at Prairie, they both mounted the graduation platform to claim their sheepskins, and to launch themselves into life. When they walked away from the exercises, they were elated but solemn, and that night, he asked Delia to be his wife.

Eleven months later, they were married.

Already they had selected their field of work. It would be among the poor people of France. Together they planned to enroll at the Emmaus Institute in Lausanne, Switzerland, to study their adopted language and to absorb the problems and dilemmas of the people they would serve. Meantime, having no money, they found interim jobs near Jim's home church in the East. To build a travel fund would take at least a year of strict economy. Skipping meals, wearing made-over clothes and darned hose, they inched toward their goal. Finally, they had saved enough for their passage and one year of tuition at the Swiss institute.

They were successful in their studies, and then a

door opened when a French-Swiss missionary group came to them with an offer. "We want you to settle in Lourdes," they said. "We have a small band of believers there who badly need a shepherd."

Jim gasped in astonishment. Lourdes was the great Catholic place of healing. Only 10 years earlier, as an 18-year-old Catholic youth, he had visited the celebrated shrine seeking God's help through the Virgin Mary. Now, he was being asked to return, of all things, as a Protestant pastor.

While his heart gave consent, his mind also thrilled at the prospect. "At last, I know what I'm to do," he thought. "Most people come to Lourdes in search of a miracle, but I shall come with the living Word of God, which can produce the greatest miracle of all—salvation, through our Lord Jesus Christ."

"You will start with a very small congregation," the mission group explained. "You may not be willing. . . ."

"How small?"

"Only eight."

Eight fellow believers in Lourdes! What a blessing and what a beginning! Jim shook himself, rejoicing. The Lord Jesus himself had begun with only twelve.

With Delia beside him, the pact was sealed. And at last the Reverend Jim Percy could commit himself to the unfolding of the life he had begun in that long-ago dream when he had told the Lord, "I'm sorry, I'm sorry, I'm sorry."

The "Mrs. America" nobody knows

ROSEMARY MURPHY HAD THE WORLD
IN HER HANDS, BUT HER HAPPINESS
WAS INCOMPLETE UNTIL SHE WON A
LARGER PRIZE, A GREATER LIFE.

"I know that face," the reporter said. "She's the girl from Indiana they elected Mrs. America."

Newsmen rarely forget a beautiful face, especially when it appears on the front page. This face belonged to a young woman sitting on the platform of the McCormick Place Auditorium in Chicago. She was looking out over the press boxes, the 40,000 persons crowding every seat, and the pulpit at which Billy Graham would soon preach.

"Her name's Rosemary Murphy," a photographer said. "Looks like a publicity stunt. Why else would a doll like her get hooked up with a revival?"

"Maybe she's a religious nut or something."

"With that face and that figure? Act your age, buddy." The newsman began to write a note.

"I'll ask for an interview. Might be a story."

Mrs. America of 1961, Rosemary Murphy of Kentland, Indiana, was hoping no one would notice her. Her busy 12-month reign was over, yet they had insisted that she take a seat of honor. In the past year, she had sat on platforms with 20 different governors, had given 150 interviews, and had appeared before club meetings, cooking schools, and home openings. Faces always crowded close, tense, pushing, seeking some special privilege.

Now she looked about the auditorium.

"What a production," she thought, "how beautifully managed."

This Chicago crusade had begun with the greatest support in midwestern history. Over 15,000 counselors had attended training classes. Prior to the opening, 2,000 Christians had visited a million homes around Chicago. Every noon, rallies were held down town at Orchestra Hall. Seven radio stations were broadcasting services to support 7,000 prayer groups that were meeting daily in homes and offices. Each night, 40,000 spectators jammed the hall. Tonight, the special guests were young gang leaders in jackets bearing such names as the Spanish Cobras, Vice Lords, Apaches, Maniacs, and the Mighty Midgets.

An usher offered her a slip of paper. She read the note with dismay. The newspaperman who sent it was an old acquaintance, seeking an interview. She sank more deeply into her chair, envying her sister and her friends sitting inconspicuously in the audience. This night of all nights she wanted to be unnoticed, not a celebrity. She was more concerned with her church affiliation and her five children who attended Sunday school regularly. Tonight, she wanted to be just herself.

Cliff Barrows was rehearsing the choir, leading them into memory hymns and choruses. She felt suddenly exalted. "I sensed a great Presence," she says, "and the song went through my mind, 'Are Ye Able?' " She shut her eyes, looking inward and praying, "Lord, only you know whether I am able, but I am willing."

Her newspaper acquaintance was waiting for an answer and she scribbled it, asking him please to forget that he had seen her. Then Billy Graham stepped to the lectern, Bible in hand.

His message was blunt, hard hitting, and seemed aimed at her heart. To her astonishment, she began to learn that the Bible had answers for some of her personal problems. She thought, "How badly I've managed my life."

It had begun promisingly in Sunday school when she was a child and continued into Youth Fellowship camps. Then she had joined the church of her parents, and gone off to Purdue University. But George Murphy, the man in her life, was impatient to get married. So she quit school in 1948, hurried to New London, Connecticut, where he was serving in the Navy, and became Mrs. Murphy. When he had served his hitch, they moved to Kentland and a fine civilian job.

The life was everything anyone could want, just as average and wonderful and frantic as that of any ideal, frantic American family. One day, a friend said, "Rosemary, you're into everything. Why not enter the home-making contest at the state fair up at Crown Point?"

"Why do a thing like that?"

"Well, they're trying to find Indiana's ideal home-maker, and they just might pick you."

"I wouldn't have a chance."

"You think about it."

She entered, and she won. "It turned out," she says, "I qualified to represent the state of Indiana at the national finals in Fort Lauderdale, Florida. There, I competed with 50 other finalists. We had to pass a series of homemaking tests. We were judged on poise, personality, and participation in community activities."

When the judges voted, Rosemary became Mrs. America.

She looked now at the sea of faces, rapt and intent, each person absorbing his own unique understanding of Graham's message.

The evangelist's strong voice wove a spell in her heart. He was speaking of God's peace. At fourteen, she thought she had captured it but it had escaped. How long ago that was. Other successes had come but not peace. Suddenly, she felt the tears coming unbidden and unexpected.

A man sitting next to her extended his handkerchief. Her tears continued, so he opened a small book and passed it along. It was the New Testament.

The sermon ended and Billy Graham gave the invitation. "Come," he said, his eyes searching the distances. She wondered what she would do if he looked at her. Would she rise? Would she dare? What would those 40,000 people think?

The reporter would make a story of it, probably, labeling it a press agent stunt. She could imagine the headline: "Mrs. America Hits Sawdust Trail—But Why?" Her lips trembled with a fresh compulsion.

"Part of me held me in my seat and said, 'You can't leave now. It's too conspicuous,'" she remembers. "The other part pulled with such a pull as I have never felt. Suddenly, I said, 'I'm going,' and I went down the steps to the front and rededicated myself to the Lord's work." Her sister, watching from among the thousands, came forward, too, to cling to her hand.

What mystery was at work in the heart of this responsible, church-going, model American homemaker? "What really happened, as I look back on it," she says, "is that I received the grace of God. I like to think this was an act of my own free will. As a mother loves and accepts a child when it is born, so Christ loves us and accepts us as we are. Whatever our ways, He says, 'Come, come as you are!' So this child came and received birth through Christ and was converted.

"After we are born, our parents begin to teach us and guide us," she adds. "And just as a child desires to please his parents because of his love for them, so does a Christian desire to please God because of his love for Christ." She had to learn these truths over a span of time.

When she was home, her minister called, notified of her rededication by the crusade's follow-up department. In the past, she had done small chores around the church. "But with a halfhearted interest," she confesses. "I sang in the choir because I enjoyed singing. It was that sort of thing."

Her minister now said, "We have so many needs, Rosemary. The junior high department needs teachers . . ."

She said, "I'll teach. What else can I do?"

Her Sunday-school class studied the letters of Paul, letters she had never once glimpsed in her entire church life. "I found his teaching to be of the greatest help," she says. "It answered so many of my questions."

Word reached her ears of the phenomenal success of the crusade she had attended. The last meeting in Soldiers Field had attracted 116,000 persons. At its conclusion, 1,735 inquirers came forward. Five nights of TV telecasts followed and an estimated 10,000,000 families listened.

In Chicago, a reporter asked Billy Graham, "What have you really accomplished? Has your crusade changed anything?"

Graham responded, "Six months from now, people will tell you that nothing has happened, but five years from now converts of this crusade will be solidly built into the church life of all this area and will be spreading the Gospel in mission fields all over the world."

Rosemary Murphy felt that she, too, was a part of that ongoing work and that it was a part of her. Her efforts in behalf of her church doubled, and so did her insights into her own dilemmas.

"One day," she explains, "I found myself sitting in our pew listening to what our minister had to say. It was a wonderful experience because I felt at last that my eyes were beginning to see and my ears were beginning to hear. I felt in touch with life. I was more sensitive to people and to my surroundings."

Her discoveries were only beginning. "When I admitted my defeat without Him, God answered me," she says. "When I confessed the sin of self-sufficiency and cried to Him for help, He gave me the Holy Spirit. When I finally stripped off all ego, He came into my life. Only through weakness do we find His strength given to us. I know, for I asked, not for God's blessing or rewards, but only for His mercy."

On Palm Sunday, after coming home from church, she received a blessing of which she had hardly dared dream. The experience was so personal and so ineffable that she can hardly describe it, but its essence was this:

"There was a wrenching and a tearing, and then there was a flood of warmth that was overpowering . . . so very much happiness filled me that I did not feel I could contain it all. At last, I felt that I was free and that I was a living vessel of Jesus Christ."

What conjoining of forces was this? "The only explanation I can give is that we do not bring God to ourselves. Whatever we receive is altogether due to His grace."

Being Mrs. America for a busy year remains a pleasant memory but Rosemary Murphy's eyes are now fastened on larger goals than this life affords. "We anticipate keenly Christ's coming," she says. "And I for one want to be at my best. I want to take the best possible care of my body, my mind, my soul, my home, my husband, my children—*because they are God's possessions.*"

What makes a successful life?

When she hears the question, Rosemary answers with a favorite quotation borrowed from Dr. Charles Malik:

Success is neither fame nor wealth nor power. Success is seeking and knowing and loving and obeying God. And if you seek, you will know, and if you know you will love, and if you love, you will obey.

Class of Harringay, '54

THESE TWO, THESE NEWBORN TWO,
SPEAK FOR THOUSANDS WHO, HAVING
HEARD THE LORD, CAN NEVER BE THE
SAME AGAIN.

If you were to stand in London's Piccadilly Circus and shout, "Harringay, 1954," a good many of the passers-by might consider you daft, but among them there almost certainly would be several men or women who would say to themselves, "Yes! Harringay in 1954; I went there then to hear Billy Graham."

And of all those who heard him then, there would be an inner circle of those who went forward in response to his invitation to lead the Christian life, to accept Jesus Christ as Lord and Master.

And of that inner circle, there would be an inner inner band whose lives were so cleansed and realigned that their labors ever since have been a manifestation, not of their own talents, but of the hand of God.

And in this faithful group, there would be a striking young woman named Yvonne Simms and a personable young man named Robert Howarth who told their thrilling stories last year in the columns of an English religious periodical called *The Christian.*

For a long time, the editors had wondered how best to answer a question so often asked about those converts of 1954. Did they mature and stand firm in the faith? Had their lives really changed? "If we could get them to talk about it," an editor said, "then the truth would finally be known."

"But will people talk? Among us British, religion is a rather private matter."

"Well, we can give them a chance."

The Christian called its series, "Harringay '54. Where Are They Now?"

Here is Yvonne Simms, speaking for herself.

London Bridge Station is a good place to start a spiritual journey. "Come and hear Billy Graham," suggested the silent poster. Why not?

For years I had had a secret prayer life which consisted of repeating lists of people to God and asking Him to bless them. There was no sense of conversing with Him, or of expecting any answers. My father had been an agnostic and my widowed mother was a backslidden Roman Catholic. I was a nominal Methodist, fairly newly married to a Jew!

At Harringay, the appeal to "decide for Christ" did not move me in the slightest. Then I seemed to hear my Christian name stated. It was not "called," but more like overhearing a calm entry in a register. My heart flashed back a horrified "No!"

On the way home, far from feeling "conviction," or

sorrow for sin, I was surrounded by a wonderful peace. I knew that this was *forgiveness*. There the matter might have ended, if that same feeling of peace had not met me again—this time, thirteen days later in the gardens of a ruined abbey at Canterbury.

That night my husband and I watched the moon sailing in and out of the clouds—often disappearing but always coming back. We never read the Bible, but there was an old one in the house. I picked it up and read a verse in Isaiah 40: "Lift up your eyes on high, and behold who hath created these things, that bringeth out their host by number: he calleth them all by names . . . for that he is strong in power; not one faileth" (v. 26). Was God talking about His moon and stars, or all those souls at Harringay?

All this time, I had not said anything to anybody, but the next day I went back to Harringay and walked to the front.

When the Holy Spirit entered my heart, He heightened every aspect of life, like a sixth sense. The Bible was lit up and I read it avidly, gladly taking advantage of all the follow-up helps sent through the post. I was also led into fellowship with Christians at the crusade office and thus to my first meeting with Christ himself. Somebody casually asked me to write out how my intellectual convictions were resolved spiritually! To one fond of secular journalism this sounded great fun, until after five days of spiritual struggle, God taught me that anything to be used for *His* glory would never come from within, but must be *received by faith from Him*. I saw that God must write it *through* me. It was then that Christ showed himself to me.

With the vision of Christ came a sudden, much

deeper insight into Scripture, and a call to service. It was not a case of consecrating a gift to Him, but of handing my writing back to Him forever, to be used only when and how He chose. I did no writing at all for nearly six years, but this never worried me, as I had been told the invitations would come from Him. And, after years of testing, they did come, exactly as He had promised!

In 1956, a very difficult family problem coincided with the birth of our baby girl, and both events were followed by a period of terrible spiritual darkness when it seemed that God had taken His Spirit completely away. During this time God taught me that without His Spirit, we can do absolutely nothing—not even understand the Bible. He taught me how to love Him more than anything or anyone else.

Meanwhile, my husband and I, through a letter in our local paper, had invited any lonely person to come to tea and to church. Forty people turned up! All were looking for God! He, knowing our weakness, did not send them all at once. They wrote, arrived, or phoned over a period of fourteen weeks. Nineteen or so came to church and six professed conversion. At this time too, a small group of us started to pray for revival. It was then that I started the habit of setting aside an hour a day for prayer and Bible reading. God has graciously allowed me to carry on with this and it has become the secret strength of my Christian life.

Suddenly the Spirit "returned." In 1958 our son was born and about this time my sister became a Christian and was baptized in the Church of England.

In 1959, my mother, who had seemed quite well, was found to have acute cancer. My sister and I shared the nursing and kept the secret from her, finding a wonderful fellowship in the Lord. Throughout the terrible pain, His presence overshadowed us all. At the end she fell asleep with her hand on God's Word. She had come back to God several months before she had died and had been received into the Church of England. (This was in answer to prayer, for there was no human persuading.) The funeral was a time of great joy and witness, for knowing our mother was happily alive with our heavenly Father, we had no sorrow at all.

Both our children have learned to pray. The little girl, aged seven, goes to Crusaders and reads her Bible every day. How quietly God's gracious influence has invaded three generations of our family! My husband is still not converted, although he is very sympathetic to spiritual things.

As for God's call, requests for articles, book reviews, and other writing come uninvited now, just as God said they would!

The means of grace which has been most valuable is the hour I spend with Him each day, for the years have taught me to expect very little from man and everything from God! He has had to teach me that Christians really are sinners and not saints, and that they must be loved with the love of God and not with human emotions. Yet one of the sweetest doctrines I know is that Christians are united to the Lord and to each other eternally and indivisibly.

Robert Howarth had to be persuaded to go to Harringay. But when a stranger asked, "Did you ever try to be an elephant?" he was jarred into an incredible adventure. This is how he tells it.

Of all our night activities in Kenya sitting in ambush was the one I enjoyed least. The most strategic places to wait were usually the coldest and dampest and hardest. Bushes and trees would suddenly become figures armed to the teeth, approaching with stealth. You couldn't talk or smoke, just think and think and think. And always disquieting questions thrust themselves up: "How do I reconcile all this—a loaded Sten gun, my finger itching to squeeze the trigger—with what I'm supposed, as a Christian, to believe? Yes, I know they are Mau Mau terrorists bent on murder, while I represent law and order. But is everything as it ought to be in my life? Am I *really* better than they? What about the hatred in my heart; the readiness to shoot first and ask questions afterwards; all the big talk and banter in the mess, as though this were not the nightmare I inwardly believe it to be . . . ?"

This was Kenya, 1953. I didn't know it then, but God was at work. I had been brought up and educated here. No stranger to the Church, I yet found myself questioning more and more the practicability and relevance of what it seemed to require of me. My best intentions for others seemed always to evaporate in the heat of personal interests!

A year later, while in London for further training, I was persuaded to hear Billy Graham at Harringay Arena. It was here, I believe for the first time in my life, that I heard the claims of Jesus Christ presented, simply and authoritatively.

At the end of his talk the speaker invited those who

wished to know more to come to the front of the auditorium. I went and was subsequently introduced to a man of my own age and we talked for a while. Then I made my way to the exit, tantalized but still in a deep fog.

Just as I was about to go out, I was confronted by a man who looked me in the eye and said:

"Are you a Christian?"

"Strange question," I thought, putting on my best Sunday-school smile and saying:

"Oh yes, I think so."

"Are you a Christian?" he insisted, a light in his eye.

"Crank," I thought. "Humor him and then escape!"

So I replied, "Well, I'm trying to be."

"Ever tried to be an elephant?"

Grinning at my dumb astonishment, he took me by the arm, sat me down in a chair and explained that no amount of trying could ever transform me into a Christian (any more than it could turn me into an elephant). Then he began to explain what New Testament Christianity was all about. That Jesus Christ had died—in *my* place. That He had paid the full penalty which *my* sins demanded. As I was, I stood condemned before a holy God; I needed a Savior. Jesus alone could save me. Forgiveness for the past was possible in Him. Moreover, in His resurrection, He was offering me power to live the sort of life I had hitherto considered hopelessly out of reach.

What a stupendous offer! If the living God were really asking to come into my wretched, tarnished life, to take over what I was only wasting and spoiling—how dare I refuse Him! He was promising:

"Behold, I stand at the door and knock: if any man

hear my voice and open the door, I will come in to him, and will sup with him, and he with Me."

I flung open the door. He was as good as His word.

This was a grand start, but what next? I recognized that I should need to become better acquainted with the Bible; that prayer and association with other Christians was important . . . but how? How does one pray? How does one read the Bible? Which church? So when I was introduced to a group of students who had come to Christ in the same way as I, and who were evidently asking the same questions, I joined them eagerly. And for the next few months we met together every week to be taught these things and others by a man who was anxious that we should spend no longer than was necessary in spiritual infancy. The discipline imposed by these associations was fierce but healthy and I am still building on the foundations of regular and systematic Bible study and memorization that were laid then. They expected high standards of faithfulness from us—for Jesus' sake—and they got them.

After finishing at college I was invited by The Navigators to go to their headquarters in the United States for a period of training. It was no ordinary Bible school or theological college, and the training was directed toward the fullest development of each individual. Not the least among the valuable lessons I learned there was the work I did in the print shop. I thought I knew more about print than any of the amateurs with whom I worked (I was a printer, after all!), but found myself occupied mostly with sweeping the floor!

Nine months later The Navigators were asked to send a team to Kenya to work amongst the thousands detained under the Mau Mau Emergency Regulations. A lot of evangelism was being carried on in these camps but there was a pressing need for the follow-up of those who had responded to the Gospel. Because of my background and familiarity with Kenya, I was asked to go with them, and this call constituted the greatest challenge of my Christian life so far. What of my career? My parents had had to sacrifice to put me through college, and now the use of my training must be suspended at least for a further period. Yet deep down, I knew that it was God, not the Navigator leader who was calling me to go.

That was eight years ago. Our work in Kenya soon changed its emphasis from Bible study correspondence courses for detainees to that of training lay leaders in the local Kikuyu churches. The same New Testament principles which helped establish me in the Christian life were patently effective in the different circumstances of Kenya.

Now God has brought me back to London, to the church which I joined soon after my conversion—All Souls, Langham Place, W.1. Here I am working among some of London's tens of thousands of visitors from overseas. We have a live and expanding International Fellowship and our aim is to win the unconverted to wholehearted allegiance to our Savior and King, and to establish those who are already Christians in their faith. We want these Christians to become effective and faithful witnesses here in Britain, especially to others from overseas, that they might return to their homes stronger in the Lord than when they came.

He was a hero but officially dead

ALCOHOL WAS LOUIS ZAMPERINI'S REAL ENEMY, UNTIL HE HEARD A MESSAGE ONE NIGHT THAT CALLED UP ALL GOD'S REINFORCEMENTS.

This account of the conversion of Louis Zamperini, of Los Angeles, may change your life. Already, his life has changed the hearts of hundreds.

He was a young Olympic athlete when he went to war and his plane crashed in the Pacific Ocean. He and one companion drifted on a life raft for 47 days, and then were rescued, only to spend two and one-half years in a Japanese prison camp. Pronounced "officially dead" he later made a triumphant return home as a war hero. Then followed a period of slow decay and demoralization of his human spirit.

Zamperini became a drinker. "In 1949," he says, "I was a well-known habitué of the bars along Hollywood Boulevard. I had forgotten the many promises I'd made to God while floating on that life raft and in Jap prisons. I lived a wild life in Hollywood. Later, I got married, but

I failed in business even when it was almost impossible to fail."

One night, his wife Cynthia talked him into attending Billy Graham's crusade in the big tent at Washington and Hill streets, following her own conversion there. Their marriage was rocky enough, he felt; now she was on this religious kick, and he started to leave during the invitation. But when he was halfway out, he heard Graham say, "When you accept Christ as your Savior, Christ will help you lead a Christian life. You turn to Him and He will uphold you."

Louis thought, "Well, I might have a chance, if I could have some help."

With help during the years since VJ day, he might have held on to some of the $10,000 in back pay he had run through, or picked more dependable business partners, or avoided some of the uncannily bad breaks that finally drove him to desperation. Graham said again: "You turn to Christ, and He will help. He'll be with you always."

So the tired, defeated hero turned around in the sawdust aisle of that crowded tent, and walked straight back to the foot of the altar. Later, in the adjoining prayer tent, a counselor stood a pointed pencil on his Bible, demonstrating how it toppled over when it was not supported, no matter how perfectly it was balanced, and then he wrapped his hand around it, holding it upright. "The pencil is you," he told Zamperini. "The hand is Christ's, which will uphold you with His righteousness."

The next day, when a thirsty Louis stood in the sun outside his favorite bar, he felt a ghostly hand on his shoulder. Abruptly, he turned away. Christians call this invisible tugging "God's leading."

Since 1949, following God's leading has been Zamperini's way of life.

He had been a hater, too. During his years in Japanese prison camps, he had been tortured and abused. Once, they had starved him and then forced the ex-Olympic miler to run through the mockery of races against Japanese athletes. Their atrocities to his body had filled his mind with hatred. But after going forward in the crusade meeting, he planned an Oriental pilgrimage to look up and apologize to the Japs he had hated most. Friends tried to dissuade him. "It's over and forgotten by everyone but you. Why waste time on such a trip?" He said, "God wants me to go."

He begged and borrowed until he raised the necessary money. The book called *Billy Graham*, written by Stanley High, completes the story.

> He sought out as many of his torturers as he could find— some of them in prison. To each he gave his Christian testimony and offered, with his hand, his friendship. "The six-year hate was over," Zamperini reported. "And I prayed my thanks . . ."

Though he had been too hotheaded and impulsive to get along with people, God now taught him patience. His schooling began when he faced his own tangled life and perceived, for the first time, that it had meaning. "When I heard the Gospel," he says, "I realized there was some reason why God had spared my life in that wartime plane crash and then in the prisoner-of-war camp. I also felt that God had allowed my long siege of hard luck to bring me to Him."

He asked God to lead him in deciding what to do with his life. The response came soon. "Having been a juvenile delinquent and a pretty hard nut to crack, I got the feeling that if receiving Christ as Savior could change me, it could change anybody. So I felt called to work with delinquent boys."

He visited Christian boys' camps, learning the art of counseling. He directed some of the early Lifeline camps for the Youth for Christ organization, of which a youthful Billy Graham had been the first international vice president. Finally, with a truck borrowed from a Japanese friend and a leased piece of land in a national forest, he opened his own Christian camp for boys from 9 to 13. "I had no credentials," he recalls, "except a deputy sheriff's badge." His bank balance was $50.

He spent two years working with younger boys, deepening his self-discipline and patience, learning to hang onto his temper, discovering the wisdom of the Bible and the power of prayer, and the art of communicating with hard-eyed toughs. Then he asked the state to send him some 16- to 18-year-old delinquents, all petty gangsters, in whom he was most interested, having nearly been one himself. California authorities picked out an unpromising crew and let him truck them off to the mountains. A state psychiatrist came along to observe.

Inevitably, the day came when a quintet of teenage thugs ran amuck and knocked the camp's code of behavior galley-west. The visiting doctor was furious. Back at the state institution, their behavior would have been punished at once. "Zamperini, you'd better handcuff those boys to trees," he demanded.

Louis was angry, too, but he held himself in check. His project hung in the balance. A quick solution would be to put the bullies in irons, but the silent voice that was always with him directed another course. "I think we'll try the Christian approach," he announced.

Presently, under the high blue sky over that California mountain camp, a new spirit settled into the hearts of the mutineers. No state officer could have achieved it, not even with the harshest discipline and punishment. One evening, the five troublemakers rose to their feet before the camp assembly. With tears filling their eyes, they apologized to their campmates for their misbehavior and promised to give no more trouble. The astonished psychiatrist rushed a report to the state capital that praised and supported everything Zamperini was doing.

Later, Louis recalls happily, another state psychiatrist came to visit his camp, and hearing the Gospel invitation one night, raised his own hand in acceptance of the Lord.

Today, Louis and his nonprofit Victory Boys' Camps are trying to fill the gap he discovered in the lives of so many renegade boys. He calls it the "thrill gap."

"I had to interview hundreds of boys before I discovered it," he says. "They were committing a variety of crimes in the state. Finally, I asked them, 'Why did you rob that gas station?' 'Why did you start on marijuana?' 'Why did you beat up the old pensioner?'

"In their replies, one element was common to all. They said, 'I did it for kicks. I did it for laughs, that's all. I did it for thrills, for excitement.'

"I began to pray, 'Lord, if that's what they want, let's start a program that will give it to them. And that was the real beginning of our Victory Boys' Camps."

Zamperini talked to an Olympic ski jumper, Keith Wageman, who agreed to work with him. Together, they found the owner of a lodge in the Mammoth Lakes area and explained their idea. He told them, "You bring your boys up here and I'll give you a week's free room and board."

It was what he had prayed for. He recalls, "We decided to set up a program of mountaineering, glacier climbing, skiing, survival, rescue, visiting ghost towns, and riding down the rivers in inner tubes.

"It worked like a charm. We had kids dangling over cliffs at the ends of ropes, and you should have seen some of those tough guys freeze with fright. But when they got down they said it was the greatest thrill of their lives. They said it was even a bigger kick than rolling a drunk or stealing a car. Today, some of them are mountaineers, some are expert skiers, and many of them are Christians."

Each summer, the boys arrive at the Victory Camp in groups of twenty-five to thirty-five. They are suspicious and on their guard. Louis says, "The first week, we don't preach. Instead, we perform. We go off a ski jump or rappel 120 feet down a vertical cliff. Each day, after we've taken them skiing or crossed a glacier or made a pack trip, we bring them back to the chalet at base camp. We have our dinner, a movie, and some songs, and then they sit around waiting for the pitch. Instead, we dismiss them with a prayer and they go to bed."

Now they really are curious. They had been told to bring Bibles, so they hang around Zamperini's door with a question that is always the same: "Hey, aren't we supposed to get some kind of religious instruction?"

"As soon as we find that their minds and hearts are beginning to open," Louis says, "we tell them about the biggest thrill of all. We present the Gospel. About the third or fourth night, we give the boys an opportunity to accept the Lord as their Savior."

Many boys have made decisions for Christ in each camp, but none is pressured. "I interview each one personally to see whether it is a real commitment. If it turns out that his action was based on some motive such as hero worship or a desire to imitate a buddy, I tell him, 'You take the rest of the week. When you are ready to receive the Lord, come back and see me.' "

Recently, the Lord led ex-bombardier Zamperini to add a flight section to his Victory Schools. All his flight camp counselors are aviators, and he borrows planes from Christian businessmen. "When my boys fly with our pilot," he explains, "and they hear him talking to the tower, and they watch him working the controls, they get excited. That pilot becomes their hero, and he commands their complete respect. They listen to every word he has to say. And while he's instructing in solo flying, he shares with them his Christian testimony. It has proved a wonderful way to reach youngsters."

What next? "When the time comes, I'll know what to do," Zamperini says.

But how does an average mortal *know*? A thousand friends have asked him, "How can you be sure?" It is difficult to explain to a non-Christian. Once, a friend put this same question to Billy Graham.

"Several things must all work together," he said. "First, you must ask God in faith to lead you, meaning that you have surrendered completely and are willing to be led. Second, God never leads contrary to Scripture, so you must check your wish against what has already been laid down in the Bible. And then God never leads against your own feeling of the rightness of things which, in us ordinary mortals, is simply called common sense."

A marvellously clear explanation is to be found in *The Christian's Secret of a Happy Life,* by Hannah Whitall Smith. She compares the relationship of God and man to that of parent and child. The parent, wanting to help, cannot do so unless the child has enough trust to cooperate. Again, the parent wanting to help, knows he could do a perfect job if only he could get into the mind of his child so as to make him *want* the same things for himself that the parent wants for him.

To discover God's leading for your own personal idea or intention or program, Mrs. Smith suggests four steps:

1. Go to the Scriptures to learn what God has already revealed. (Do this daily, until knowledge of these principles becomes your second nature.)

2. With reference to whatever you feel led to undertake, see if "a way opens," as the Quakers put it, for its accomplishment. (When Zamperini first thought of returning to Japan, a "way opened" when friends advanced him expense money. Mrs. Smith calls these providential circumstances.)

3. What does your mind say you ought to do? What is your "impression"? Here, one can get into trouble. Wrong impressions will come from bad health, from bad advice, whether from friends or relatives, or from spiritual enemies. The ultimate test, as Billy Graham said, is accord with your own common sense. God never leads against common sense.

4. Are the three previous tests all in harmony? Does your innermost sensitivity sense a block or check any-

where? If so, wait for it to be removed. If not, do you have a sense of "oughtness"?

If this feeling of "oughtness" fails to come, Mrs. Smith says, "Wait." If it does come, in faith obey immediately.

She cites the Apostle John: "He calleth his own sheep by name . . . and he goeth before them, and the sheep follow him."

She says to notice here the expressions, "goeth before" and "follow." God goes before to open a way, and we are to follow in the way thus opened.

Louis Zamperini spent many years learning that going his own way, riding roughshod toward his own goal, led only to tragic failure. But when he let the Lord "go before," he learned that doors opened everywhere.

Because they opened, countless California youths have been regenerated. "And it is interesting to note what this program has done for me personally," he adds. "When I was first converted, I felt like an old man. Today I go skiing with college boys who quit by two o'clock. I stay out until the lift closes, then climb the mountain for another hour or two and ski down. I'm 46 years old but I expect to be skiing when I'm 70. My work keeps me in shape all year round." Thus, a man's once-sodden body changes.

And his spirit? "That illustration of the hand and the pencil, given to me 15 years ago, still holds. God really will hold up a man who turns to Him and asks to be held up. Certainly what happened in that crusade tent was the greatest lesson of my life. Of course, there have been trying periods. It's like running the mile. That is not pleasure, really. It can be torture. Yet, the victory at the end is always worth it. It's the same way in climbing a mountain or crossing a glacier. When you get to the top you say, 'Man, all this is worth the struggle.'

"And the greatest thing of all has been that Jesus Christ was with me all the way."

God's hot pursuit

SOME CALL IT FATE OR LADY LUCK, BUT THE WORBOYS' LEARNED THERE IS NO ESCAPE WHEN GOD POINTS HIS FINGER.

"I'm too shy," she told herself, and walked away from the meeting she wanted to attend. "I'm too shy," she confessed, and turned away from the strangers she wanted to meet. "I'm too shy," she whined into her pillow, sobbing because she was lonely and unwanted and life was passing her by.

All her life, Phyllis had used the excuse. It was a crutch to defend her isolation. She might have used it all the remainder of her listless life except that God was in hot pursuit.

She could not know, nor even suspect that He had a plan for her but in the end it became crystal clear.

Living in England as a girl, she remembers, "I was never at rest. Nothing seemed secure. And then I discovered dancing. From my 16th birthday on, dancing was the joy of my life. But my only friends were other girls who enjoyed dancing, too."

She wanted to see the world. Despite her timidity with strangers, her restlessness drove her to find jobs that would roll back the horizon. She finally found work in South America.

In Buenos Aires, she fell in love with Arthur Worboys, a railway signals engineer. Their marriage followed but World War II cut short their honeymoon.

Arthur hurried back to England to be commissioned in His Majesty's Armed Forces. Phyllis joined the women's army of the Royal Air Force.

Thus began the six most miserable years she was ever to know. While he served in India, Burma, Ceylon, and Australia, she learned to live alone. "It was the off-duty times that were so bad," she says. "I missed my husband. My shyness was such that I made only a few friends. How lonely life can be even amongst a lot of people!"

At her camp, church services were conducted by a chaplain and by Salvation Army officers. "I'll talk to them," she vowed to herself, but when the moment came she always fled. Loneliness closed in tighter than ever. "I tried going to different churches in London," she says, "but they didn't touch me at all."

The war's end brought Arthur home and they sailed back to Argentina to complete his contract with the railways. Now they were both different people, and the old excitement of seeing the world had worn thin. By 1948, they were back in England, looking for work.

Postwar England was a dreary place with two men for every job, and gaping bombed-out areas scarring the cities. She does not like to remember the grim particulars.

"We passed through our most difficult time," she says. "Both of us were worried and distressed. The future seemed very dark."

The notion of God's pursuit of them, had it occurred then, would have seemed more malevolent than benign. But it became barely visible to the naked eye on the day they moved into a flat next to the Redcliffe Women's Missionary College in London. This institution, devoted to preparing young ladies for Christian service, was managed by a staff of greathearted women.

Phyllis Worboys walked timidly through the neighborhood, learning its features. She observed the students, heard their laughter, and was secretly envious of their happiness. "I wish I could get acquainted with them," she thought, and then fled down the roadway as if the devil were chasing her.

One day as she strolled, a stranger planted herself in her path. Phyllis had seen her at the college door and knew she was a high official. "I've watched you in this neighborhood," she said "and you're always alone."

"We moved here just recently," Phyllis said.

"Never mind that. I want you to come over and have tea with us at Redcliffe."

"Oh, thanks! I'd love to come over some day."

There it was again, that escape clause boring into her intentions. Some day, eh? She knew what that meant. It meant never.

Hating herself for her shyness, longing for friendship, she kept away. Months passed. One day, the same kindly lady charged across the pavement at her, smiling and bright-eyed, as if Phyllis were the answer to a prayer.

"I know you can help me," she said. "I need some

sewing work done in the college. Have you any idea who might do it?"

"Oh, I could do it," Phyllis said, before she thought. Off stage somewhere, a voice whispered, "Contact."

So she went to the college and met her neighbors. Through them, she began to attend a weekly meeting of Christian women directed by an extraordinary leader, Mrs. Gunn. Here, more friendships were formed, but more important, Phyllis began to appreciate the value of Bible study.

One day Mrs. Gunn had a special message. "It was about SIN, in big capital letters. My mind wandered a bit at first, and then those three letters hit me full in the face. I can remember how startled I was. They were surely directed right at me and they hit the target. I knew I had to talk more to Mrs. Gunn."

Presently, Phyllis Worboys received Jesus Christ as her Savior.

She did not tell Arthur. "But you must tell him," her new friends insisted.

She argued, "He won't understand and I don't want to disturb him. He's working all hours trying to get started in a new line. It's very trying for him. He's got enough troubles."

"You have to tell him," they ordered.

Arthur came home that night and they had dinner. Later, after pussyfooting all around the subject, she screwed up her courage and explained what she had done. He nodded enigmatically, and gave a little smile. Nothing more. She wondered what he was thinking.

"He knew that the only Bible I possessed had very small print," she remembers. "Two days later he brought me a surprise, a new Bible I could read more easily."

100

Billy Graham's appeal to young people has always been universal.
Here he listens intently as teen-agers question him on matters of
faith. *Photo by Russ Busby.*

Billy Graham addressing the First Youth Night crusade at the Los Angeles Coliseum, August 19, 1963, in which 3,216 persons came forward.

Long a friend of the leaders of State, Graham is welcomed by the late President John F. Kennedy at the White House. *Photo by Seth Muse.*

There are always a great many young people who feel the inspiration of Billy Graham's sermons and come forward at each meeting. *Photo by Russ Busby.*

Thousands of people, white and black, sit on the ground to hear the American evangelist during his African tour of 1960.

A counselor reads the Bible to an intense group of young people. *Photo by Russ Busby*.

Great crowds were on hand to welcome Billy Graham at the airport at Sao Paulo, Brazil, on his arrival there to begin his crusade. *Photo by Russ Busby*.

Thousands listen raptly during Billy Graham's appearance in Lima, Peru, in 1962. *Photo by Russ Busby.*

The turnout in Copenhagen, Denmark, was unprecedented for that small country during Graham's crusade in 1965. *Photo by Russ Busby.*

An historic moment when the nation's political leaders heard Billy Graham. On the far left is the late President John F. Kennedy, and on the far right is President Lyndon B. Johnson. *Photo by Russ Busby.*

The crowd at Billy Graham's crusade in the Los Angeles Coliseum

Africans in their native dress swarm to hear Graham during his
crusade in 1960.

emphasizes the tremendous personal magnetism of the man. *Photo by Russ Busby.*

Young and old respond to Billy Graham's message, and the young people enter as fervently into the services as do their elders. *Photo by Russ Busby.*

Even in a largely Catholic country such as Venezuela, the response to Graham was tremendous. Part of the crowd who gathered to hear him in Caracas in 1962, is seen here. *Photo by Russ Busby.*

Mrs. Gunn personally set God's next snare. "Billy Graham is going to preach at Wembley Stadium," she told Phyllis. "We'll all go and hear him."

Arthur would have none of it. "You go. I'll stay home and listen on the wireless."

Mrs. Gunn would not be put off. "You bring that man over here for dinner. And leave Arthur to my husband."

You set up the dominos, and then knock one down. . . .

After dinner, the ladies retired to the kitchen leaving the men to talk. When they joined up later, Mr. Gunn said, "Phyllis, Arthur is interested in seeing the organization of the Graham campaign at Wembley. He says he can go with us on Wednesday night. Okay with you?"

Silently, she cried, "Hallelujah!"

Billy Graham's text was John 14:1. "Let not your heart be troubled: ye believe in God, believe also in me."

"It brought me such peace," Phyllis says. "I longed to go forward at the invitation but Arthur was sitting beside me stiff as a ramrod. We did nothing. The Gunns asked if we would like to go another night. Because of interruptions, the matter was not settled. I wanted to go to another meeting to make my conversion public."

So the week of the crusade at Wembley wore on until it was Friday. Phyllis begged her husband to take her again. "No, no, no," he said. Then, seeing her face, "All right, all right," he relented, "but you tell the Gunns and the others at Redcliffe that *I am not going out in front.*" From the set of his jaw, she knew that his mind was fixed.

"I left the table and dashed off to the college," she says. "The Gunns were on the rug in front of the fire

101

having coffee. When I gave them my husband's message, they said, 'Don't you worry! Just empty your heart and listen. The whole college has been praying for Arthur.' "

Their seats were very high up, and Arthur knew that his wife intended to go forward. "It's a long way down there," he told her. "I'll see you to the bottom of the steps and then wait there for you."

During the sermon, rain began to fall. By the time of the invitation, it was pouring. She pulled her raincoat around her. Arthur stood up and held out his hand. "Come on," he said. She looked into his eyes, hoping.

"He smiled, and I knew," she says. "We went down together, all the way."

How the Lord's dominos began to topple. . . .

Arthur resigned from his job and joined Victor Gunn in the Children's Special Services Mission. Shortly, an offer of a railway job came from Bolivia. They moved to La Paz, 12,000 feet above the sea and the highest national capital in the world. The La Paz Community Church elected him its chief usher. In the country's second largest city, Cochabamba, Arthur moved in to help when the pastor fell ill, and his skill at management was quickly evident. The church of ten members grew to forty while he filled its pulpit.

Back in La Paz, a religious group needed a recording engineer for a weekly broadcast. "Try Art Worboys," a worker said. "He can do anything."

Arthur recalls, "It was not long before 'Uncle John,' as I was known, took over the children's corner of the service, and later gave many of the principal messages."

In the meantime, Phyllis had been teaching groups of children and teenagers. Together, they sponsored an adult Sunday class in Spanish and watched it grow. And then the government took over the railroads and Arthur's job with it.

If there was ever a time for dropping away, for returning to the old life, it was then, because they were compelled to return to England without prospects of any kind. Old friends rallied round, heard their stories of missionary work in South America, and sent them on speaking tours.

One such tour called them to Jamaica, and the Worboys began to speak and testify throughout the island. A hurricane whirled across the gulf and hundreds of refugees huddled in a church. "It was my privilege to speak words of comfort from the twenty-third Psalm," Arthur remembers.

Phyllis started a teenagers' group in Bible study there, and mobilized a class of children for primary lessons. Her former timidity was gone. Together, they worked with committees to organize nights of prayer for world revival.

When that job was finished, they limped home again. What now? In England, they listened to the best preachers they could find, and tried to improve their own lectures. Slowly, their small fame began to grow. Counseling and speaking, they began to influence many lives.

A letter came from Bolivia. "They're building a new church in Cala Cala," Phyllis told her husband. "If we were out there, they'd turn it over to our mission."

"But we're not there," he said.

"Maybe we ought to be."

"That's a long trip—and a lot of money."

They paid their own way back to Cala Cala, and

supervised the completion of the church. One day, she told him, "Guess what?"

"What?"

"Billy Graham is coming to South America!"

They rejoiced, hardly daring to believe it.

"I've got a surprise, too," he said. "They want me back on the Bolivian Railroad."

Soon, Billy Graham began his unprecedented crusade in South America. In Bolivia, countless committees were quickly formed and projects initiated. Swiftly, the country's churches were mobilized to support meetings in La Paz, Cochabamba, Santa Cruz, and Oruro. A finance director was appointed to raise money: Arthur Worboys. Three days before the La Paz crusade, a crisis required the selection of a new director of counseling: Arthur Worboys. Phyllis organized prayer groups and youth delegations, and counseled the younger children.

One night, the mountainside facing La Paz blazed with oil drums placed to spell out words 35 feet tall. They could be read for miles. They said, "Solo Christo Salva"— "Only Christ Saves." It was the crusade's opening. Billy Graham did not see it, for he was ill, but he sent a member of his team, a missionary evangelist named Fernando Vangioni, of Buenos Aires, who preached to unprecedented crowds. More than 1,000 persons came forward.

When the crusade was over, the busy Worboys turned to other projects. Phyllis had already started writing a concordance of five New Testament books in Lowland Spanish, a language missionaries could use among Indian tribes. Arthur worked for the railroad and in the church wherever he was needed. The Holy Spirit, he had discovered, would somehow give him the time and strength needed.

They both continued to pray that the Holy Spirit would guide them to their ultimate heart's desire, which was full-time work for the Lord. How long had it been since they walked down that aisle at Wembley? How many oceans had they since crossed? Who in England in 1954 would have dreamed that the spark ignited by a sermon in a sports stadium would burst into flame on a Bolivian mountainside in the 1960's? Who could doubt that, in God's own time, it would blaze forth again?

The Worboys were not impatient. With God, you learn to wait; it is the price of exaltation.

They said, "Your life is running out"

HER VOICE WAS A WHISPER, HER
LUNGS WERE SPENT, BUT A MOMENT
OF GRACE SENT HER INTO AN AMAZ-
ING CAREER OF SERVICE TO CHILDREN.

Mary Newell had been in surgery for five hours. They had brought her into the hospital, a slender, wispy young woman too small for her twenty-odd years, but giving off an inner radiance that lighted up the corridors like a torch. Despite the hum of elevators and the clanging of utensils, nurses and fellow patients had heard her hacking cough. For years hemorrhages had drained away her vitality. Now, the famous Charlestown surgeon was removing a piece of lung afflicted with bronchiectasis.

"I don't see how she stands it," her floor nurse said.

Back in the countryside beyond Leon, West Virginia, her neighbors who knew her best had their own answer. "The kid never quits," they said. "She's a tiger."

They wheeled her, silent and white, down the hallway into the recovery room, and into the hands of God.

She still recalls the moment of awaking. Earlier,

107

she had asked God to help her through the ordeal, and to use her in Christ's ministry. "People watch a Christian when he gets in a pinch, and are ready to criticize if he doesn't measure up," she says. "I prayed that Jesus would give me the strength to show them a real, deep trust in Him."

An amazing feeling possessed her almost as soon as she uttered her prayer. "My heart was filled to overflowing with peace and joy," she says. "I knew that I was going to have something wonderful to look forward to, even if I never survived the surgery."

She awoke about five o'clock. "I was instantly wide awake and able to talk," Mary remembers. "My nurse was writing at her desk, unaware that I was conscious. I was surprised to see that I was in the recovery room. The greatest shock of all . . . I was without pain. Except for the tight feeling of the bandages that covered my chest, I wasn't even uncomfortable. I'd known there would be oxygen tubes in my nose when I woke, so I was expecting them."

The nurse rose and came quickly to the bedside. Patients coming out of anesthesia were apt to "cut a shine." Other white-clad persons gathered nearby, poised for action. Mary smiled at them, and her glow filled the room.

"How do you feel?" someone asked.

"I wanted to shout, to sing out," she remembers. "I said, 'It was nothing . . . the operation was, really, almost nothing.'" The attendants glanced at each other, unbelieving. No comparable lung case had ever been so calm or so joyous. Presently, they put Mary back to sleep, and went about their duties talking of the miracle.

"I'd told nobody I was a Christian but the whole staff knew it in a day or so," she remembers. "One old nurse came in and said, 'In all you do, do *all* to the glory of the Lord.'" Lying in bed, she tried to sort out the meaning of what was happening. "I was amazed," she says, "that a nobody like me would be used to show others the power of the Lord to help a person. I'd never expected to have any such experience as this."

The mysterious forces resulting in conversion and conviction had worked sluggishly for many years in Mary Newell's life. Faith was not served to her on a silver platter. Instead, she endured long periods of confusion and fear and utter failure. Time and again, she would reach upward with all her strength, only to collapse under the weight of ignorance.

Not all the great cataclysms of this earth are reflected by headlines about exploding volcanos or raging wars. Often, they are emotional riptides in the hearts of struggling men and women. Mary was born with many talents including music, needlecraft, and a special sensitivity to others, particularly children. But she had been born also with the incurable affliction which would finally devastate much of both her lungs.

So, in the passing years, her progress from repentant sinner to the girl whose Christian spirit stunned both friends and a hospital staff was less of a sudden explosion of light than a perilous and murky campaign against foes named jealousy, selfishness, and pride.

Billy Graham tells his crusade audiences that they can win their personal struggles by surrendering to the Master. "Just get up out of your seat and come forward.

This is your moment with God. You need Christ. You come!"

Mary "went forward" three times, meaning it with all her heart, yearning for the healing that Christ offered.

The lives of some new Christians can be compared to stepping into an elevator; almost immediately, the doors of their new life clang shut around them and they are lifted to new levels of service and happiness. Others are not so fortunate. Their progress is like that of an adventurer crossing a stream on slippery stepping stones. Mary's life was like that.

Her childhood Christian training was almost non-existent. Her parents were good people, but not Christians. They gave her illustrated books of Bible stories. They held her up to a picture of Jesus and taught her to point a finger and say, "That's the good man." But of prayer, of Bible study, of family worship, she knew nothing.

Yet, a zeal to know more about the Good Man gradually became an ever-present reality. As she grew older, ministers would give the invitation in churches she attended, and time and again she would be almost at the point of accepting, even with tears flowing down her cheeks, but always something in her kept saying, "I'll wait till I'm older." So the moment always passed.

Yet she felt a deep love for religious literature and particularly for religious music, to which she turned with youthful skill when she taught herself to play the piano. A Chinese Christian, had she known any, would have repeated to her the legend which says that every human being is born with a vacuum inside, and that a person becomes complete only when that vacuum is filled with God.

She tried to fill her vacuum with school activities and music and friends, but presently a weakness of body began to set her apart. Her parents worried, saying, "You must rest more. You're wearing yourself out." She fought them: "I'm only doing what everyone else is doing."

Confused and rebellious, she fled to her room, thinking, "They don't want me to have fun. They don't understand me at all."

The tension increased until, on a rainy night in April, 1950, Mary faced her moment of truth. "A severe lung hemorrhage struck me down, and for many hours it seemed I couldn't live. I prayed for once in my life and I meant every word. I promised if my life was spared, I would be a Christian."

She grew better. The months passed and she knew that she had not kept her promise. If her conscience pricked a little deeper with each passing month, she shrugged it off. "Religion is for old folks," she said.

The showdown came that autumn. She remembers, "A new minister came to our church and the first thing he did was to start trying to talk to me about my soul." When he opened a revival meeting that fall, she knew that her position as piano player would trap her into listening to his appeals. So she stayed home. For two nights, the services had no music, and the pricking of her conscience became as steady as a toothache.

"Mother marched me back to church," Mary recalls, "with the result that *she* was saved that week." And finally, young Mary became "so miserable that I gave up, forgetting everything except getting right with God. When I started up the aisle that evening, tears were streaming down my face until I could hardly see."

The well-wishers and back-patters came crowding around with advice and congratulations, while Mary stood, almost holding her breath, waiting for the great illumination that was to confirm her acceptance into the Kingdom. "I had heard others tell of seeing a great shining light around them. I thought I had to *feel* saved. I kept waiting for something to happen and nothing did."

Confused and vexed, she wondered if God was rejecting her. An old man came to her, holding an open Bible. "Read this," he suggested, pointing to Romans 10:9. She skimmed it, disappointed and upset.

Though she felt no enlightenment, she felt many other things. "All that night, I could not rest," she recalls, "and the next day was no better." She thought of the old man's Bible verse. She looked up Romans 10:9, and read it over. Two phrases stood out: "If thou shalt believe in thine heart . . . thou shalt be saved."

After a time, she went to another revival service, persuaded by her mother. "I stuck to my seat like a burr," she says. "But I realized that I had to do something fast." She went back to Romans 10:9 and reread it a hundred times. "Suddenly, the answer came to me. I went back to church that night ready to give up. The minister came up to me as soon as he gave the invitation, and I stepped out into the aisle with him, and just a few moments later I was on my knees at the altar. That night, salvation was mine, and finally there was joy and peace in my heart."

As is often the case, the stepping stones are slippery. Mary longed for the far shore but her feeling of gaining it

112

was soon diluted. Early in the revival, she had asked a new member of the church to substitute for her at the piano. The newcomer performed so well that she was invited to continue. Presently, Mary found herself sitting on the sidelines. When she did play, plagued by worry and nervousness, she made blunder after blunder.

"I should have blamed myself, but I didn't," she admits. "Feeling that I was a nuisance, the day came when I reached the end of my string and I quit completely."

She walked into her private valley of despair, not knowing what to do, not even suspecting that a new Christian needs the support of a quiet time for prayer, of regular Bible study, and of regular worship in God's house. Three long, painful years passed before she returned to church.

During that time, each month brought its own agony. Her absence was noted and rumors sped through the community, guessing at her motives. She disregarded them, refusing to explain. If God rejected her talent, let God's will be done. Sinking into self-pity, her health broke.

"I was filled with regret for the happiness I had lost. I longed for the fellowship of Christians, but I was too stubborn to admit I had been wrong. I put the blame for my fall completely on others. I vowed to myself that should I ever attend that church again, nobody would ever see me go to my knees and admit I was wrong."

The Bible reveals many moments and many actions which no human can understand, and so does life. In that West Virginia countryside, there came now a moment like some of those in Galilee.

Mary says, "Father took me in the car to a nearby

113

home where he left me in care of a friend. Her daughter-in-law was going to Sunday school. She asked if I wanted to go. I fairly jumped at the chance. Sickness had taken a lot of the starch out of me, and I was ready to be friends again."

So for the first time in many months, she went to the old church and attended Sunday school. It was a heart-warming morning, with old friends voicing a welcome, including the gentleman who had shown her a passage in Romans.

"I've been praying every day for you," he said.

That summer, the pastor resigned and a new one was called. Mary says, "That autumn I attended church for the first time in three years. We, my parents and brother and I, went to hear the new preacher. I took one look at him and disliked him more than any person I had ever met."

That could have been the end for Mary, except that a book came into her hands entitled "Secret of Happiness," and its author was Billy Graham. It was a slim book, bound in blue, and its final paragraph offered a special message. "It must be God speaking to me," Mary thought. For Billy Graham's last words added something new to her concept of religion. You, too, can find happiness, he said, "but you will never find it by searching directly for it. As the Lord of happiness said, 'Seek ye first the kingdom of God, and His righteousness; and all these things shall be added unto you.'"

She had wanted to play the piano, to do good, to be useful and needed. That approach was wrong. The book said, "You cannot *work* your way toward happiness and heaven, you cannot moralize your way, you cannot reform

114

your way, you cannot buy your way. *It comes as a gift of God through Christ.*"

She read, "Happy is the man who has learned the secret of coming to God daily in prayer. Fifteen minutes alone with God, every morning before you start the day, can change circumstances and remove mountains."

"I had heard Billy Graham preach once for just a few minutes during a newsreel," she says. "As I read, the same strange power swept over me that I had felt before. Things I had longed to know were being answered for me. I had been afraid to ask the questions because I feared older Christians would laugh."

Picking up a newspaper one day, she read that television would carry some of the meetings of Billy Graham's crusade in New York's Madison Square Garden.

"You must hear him. You simply must!" her inner voice urged. The station was distant, too far to transmit a picture, but from previous experience she knew that the words would be clear.

As the TV warmed, the sound of the giant crusade choir filled the room. She sank back, suddenly happy. For once, she thought, she would hear a sermon without some one tugging at her sleeve, trying to get her to go forward again. "Twice is enough," she mused. Beverly Shea began to sing, supported by the choir, and her breath choked her; it was the most beautiful music she had ever heard. Then a new voice replaced the hymn. She recognized it and glanced toward the set.

The tube was aglow with the image of Billy Graham. "It was the first time our TV set had ever brought in a picture from that station," she says today, amazement still in her quiet voice.

What an evening that was. "I forgot everything. The words struck so straight to my heart that I was completely unaware of anything going on around me. Growing in me, I felt the desire to have the kind of faith he was preaching. Within two minutes, I had turned from the girl who didn't want to admit she was wrong to one with the deepest desire to have lasting faith. When he gave the invitation, I wished with all my heart that I could have been in the New York Garden, to join those going forth to make their decisions."

On other nights, she watched again, storing up new thoughts of Christian life. Her grandfather died suddenly, then, reminding her of her own poor health. So many emotions crowded into her heart that her mother finally said, "Why don't you sit down and write Billy Graham all about it?"

She was aghast. "Me, write Billy Graham!" But she recalled that he had invited letters from his listeners, and was offering them a special recording of "How Great Thou Art."

She went to her typewriter, suddenly shy. She wrote a letter, then tore it up. Then she began anew, holding to the thought: "I'll write just as I would speak if I were to meet Mr. Graham in person."

"The words came to my mind so swiftly that I could hardly keep up with my machine," she says. "Something seemed to break within me and I made a full confession on paper."

The letter was mailed and presently forgotten. At home, she began to attend church services almost fanatically. If there had been daily services, "I would have gone," she remembers.

Then illness struck again and bad hemorrhaging began. They rushed her to a hospital. The thought of surgery brought panic. Traveling the miles between home and hospital, over rough dirt roads and slick pavements, she felt perspiration wet her face, cold as ice. The motor shook her eardrums, pounded her mind. Her only comfort was the desperate refrain of her entreaty. "Help me, Master! Oh, help me."

At the hospital, the doctor took her hands in his. "You're all right, Mary. We won't have to operate."

So she came home after a while and presently her cheeks were rounder and her spirits were higher than for months. A few days later, the mail brought a long delayed response to her letter of confession to Billy Graham, written by a special counselor in the Billy Graham team headquarters. He begged her to "let Jesus come into her heart." True to habit, she responded with anger. Nobody could tell her when to come to the Lord. Nobody could press her to a public confession.

Several nights later, Billy Graham preached another TV sermon. A backslider, he said, was like a man who fell into a ditch and was too lazy to climb out. Calmer now, she accepted his pointed charge. She said, "Okay, I'm a backslider. So I've got to climb out." She would begin sooner than she imagined.

Before dawn, her mother was rushed off to the hospital for an emergency operation. "I was physically unable to carry on her work, but I knew I had to do it," she says. "I never had realized how much I leaned on her when things went wrong. I saw the lesson in this and I asked God for strength to see me through."

Now, she worked harder than in all her life, her

weak body held together by a power she had never known. One night, she awoke from an exhausted sleep to hear unpremeditated words pouring from her lips. It was as if her purest thoughts and desires were suddenly rising through muddy waters. "I awoke in prayer," she says, "and the words I was saying promised my whole being to Christ."

Her mother returned home safe and sound, and presently a fresh revival began in Mary's little church. Night after night, she listened to the preaching of the minister whose appearance had offended her. Night after night, she held back. Pride, pride, pride . . . she uttered the word a thousand times, trying to push it away. But she went again on another night. "I was the first one down the aisle," she recalls. "Yes, I finally did kneel in the same place in front of my old friends and the minister I disliked so much."

Again, they came to her, but now a different Mary received them. This Mary had surrendered her life to God's will. The long, long trail to the altar had been traversed. She thanked them gratefully for their good wishes.

At last she had entered in, not through works but through what Hannah Smith has called consecration.

Not long ago, Mary Newell underwent a second lung operation, one made necessary by the advance of the disease in her other lung. The memory of it still scares her a little.

"Things didn't go so well this time," she says. "I was often out of my head. The first time I came to my senses, I knew I was beyond medical help. So I told Jesus, if I was to get well, it was all up to him."

118

A minister who came to visit one of her roommates began to talk to her. "Our church is praying for you," he said one day. Soon after, she recalls, her fever broke. Then came a period when everything went wrong. Her weight dropped to 82 pounds. On that Sunday afternoon he said, "Tonight, we're going to have special prayers for you."

She went to sleep, hugging that thought, and in the morning she began to mend.

Back home after a while, she sought ways of serving others. Parts of two lungs had been removed, but she learned to live with what was left.

"I've learned a new way of life," she says. "For the last three years, I've had a junior choir at church and they've more than made up for the family I will never have. The children are wonderful little fellows and how they love to learn about Jesus."

Last year, friends gave her a slide film projector and she gives shows to children's groups, both at church and in her home. Limited lung capacity prevents her from speaking without running out of breath, but the slide films, which come from a nearby religious bookstore, explain themselves, and she operates the machine—as she plays the piano—with self-taught expertness.

Determined to help support herself, she planned to go to school. When her second operation prevented this, the state gave her an electric sewing machine and a home course in needlecraft. After a few trials, she discovered that she was an expert seamstress. The word spread, bringing more orders than she could deliver. Today, despite all her handicaps, she has a paying business and is self-employed.

Sometimes, she wonders why it took so long to change her ways, to conquer the pride that held her aloof from others. She marvels, too, at the divine persistence which offered her chance after chance.

At least four of Graham's evangelistic ministries were involved: his big city crusade, its outreach via TV, books, and direct mail from a counselor. People have told Billy Graham, "You ought to take it easy. Why do you keep undertaking these new projects?" The possibility of saving a single soul like Mary Newell's is one answer.

Mary still lives on a remote road that is rutted in the winter and dusty in the summer, but her life is no longer barren or hopeless. "I go to Sunday school regularly, and to the Creston church near here whenever I can, and I enjoy being with my Christian friends," she says. "As for the future, even with this last surgery, I can live only for a short time, but I mean to make every day count instead of crying because my life is running out. Oh, did I say running out? Not for me, it isn't. For me, it's only just beginning."

An antidote for jealousy

A GERMAN BOY AND GIRL, SEPARATED BY THE IRON CURTAIN, FLEE FROM THEIR RUBBLED WORLD TO CANADA, WHERE THEY FIRST FIND HEART-BREAK, THEN A NEW LIFE.

"Be glad this didn't happen to you!"

With those words, the reader in the Minneapolis headquarters tossed a dozen blue sheets of paper to a secretary. They were addressed to Billy Graham and covered by regular, slanted Teutonic-looking script sentences. The signature read "Heintz Pellmann."

Reading those pages later, I found in their painful paragraphs the story of Everyman. Pellmann had been the boy idealist in Adolph Hitler's Jugend corps, the seeker after knowledge, the tireless worker, the East German emigrant seeking liberty, even a counterfeit Christian, in his drive toward understanding who he was. In turn, he saw every goal that he valued perverted and destroyed, and every ideal smashed. For years, he could find no remedy for his failure, nor could his loving wife help him until, one night, in her agony, she picked up an old Bible. . . .

The story really begins the night young Heintz tried to slip through the Iron Curtain. In those days, fugitive East Germans followed guides along secret paths to freedom in the West. Heintz was one of a group making its dangerous way to the northern port of Hamburg. The moon was bright, lacing the forest with shadows and silver. Their steps made a soft crunching in the leaves. A few yards more and they would cross no man's land to West Germany and freedom. Nearby, a train rumbled through.

When it had gone, Heintz hunched his tense young shoulders, making himself small. His thoughts were on tomorrow, and the years after tomorrow, when he would be a famous chef, happily married, rich and powerful. It seemed very simple, if one worked hard, improved oneself at every opportunity and kept both eyes on the main chance. . . . A rotten branch popped beneath his heel, and someone said, "Shhhhh!" Close ahead, dogs began to bark. Suddenly, a voice cried, "Halt!"

Beyond the border point named Helmstedt, in an apartment on a narrow street in moon-drenched Hamburg, a blonde girl pressed her cheeks curiously to a window, wondering if this might be the night he would come. He had written, cautiously hinting that he might slip through the curtain soon, and when he had found work, they could be married.

Their romance had begun when Allied bombers forced the school children of Hamburg to seek safety elsewhere and she was evacuated to his home town in Saxony. After the war, they had written regularly and devotedly. From the first, she had seen him as her ideal, tall and intelligent, and touchingly without guile.

Gertrude remembered how he had straggled home at the end of the war. The German nation was in collapse, with Allied troops holding complete command. "Our armies were disintegrating," he had confessed, "and so were all the ideals we had followed. Nothing was left but emptiness and loneliness."

Now, Heintz saw two immense figures standing in the shadows ahead, machine guns in their hands. Their police dogs strained at leather leashes. The refugees stopped suddenly, trapped in the flood of moonlight.

"Move over to that railway trestle," a guard ordered.

The group shuffled toward the shadowy roadbed, edging into a cul-de-sac. Suddenly, several refugees darted from their column into the shadows, and one soldier sprinted after them, screaming, "Halt! or I'll shoot!" The other man pointed his weapon straight at the group. "Back yourselves in there," he ordered, motioning with his gun. A shot exploded nearby, and the women and children cried out in fear.

Heintz saw the moon shining brightly beyond the guard's head, and his heart leaped. A cloud no bigger than a house was racing toward it. The bushes beside the embankment, he noted, were high enough to hide his body. Swift as the turning off of a floodlight, the cloud covered the moon and Heintz moved noiselessly, melting into the vegetation, edging softly toward nearby trees.

The darkness would not last long. Crawling through underbrush, he dropped into a small creek. "Lord, please help me!" he breathed.

A silhouette ahead showed the outlines of a build-

125

ing. He plunged toward it, falling through the empty doorway of an abandoned brick plant. Gasping, he watched the night outside turn bright as the cloud passed on.

Resting a while, he estimated his position. No man's land seemed to lie just over the rise to the west. He moved out cautiously and ran into a cliff rising almost vertically; it was the side of a rock quarry. Guards would be at each end, he reasoned, so he scaled the rocky face, handhold by handhold. Finally, he lay astride the crest, looking over the empty space beyond which lay West Germany. Crawling slowly and painfully, he inched toward distant lights, while behind, the sound of fading barks and whistling trains subsided. It was nearly dawn as Heintz crossed the border at Helmstedt, and asked the way to Hamburg where Gertrude waited.

Their wedding in a Lutheran church in Hamburg-Horn was simple and sweet, continuing the fairy story of their youthful romance.

Presently Heintz found work in a good profession, as a novice chef. He was very confident about what he had to do. First, you decide what you want. "I want success," he told himself. "Getting ahead is very important to me."

"Heintz, what's your idea of success?" asked his friends.

"I want to become a famous chef. And I want to improve myself in every way I can." He spoke up loudly, but underneath he was very unsure.

He and Gertrude studied thick books, reading all the philosophies that flourished in postwar Germany. They enrolled in evening courses in character building, in positive thinking, and even in astrology. When these failed to satisfy, he looked up other evening courses, so many that they merged and blurred, and still he came no closer to his goal.

Next, he turned to reading, hour after hour, living in fear that someone would ask a question which he could not answer. With Gertrude, he studied archeology, astronomy, art, evolution, physics. . . .

During those years, Gertrude bore two baby boys, cute and blond, and apparently sufficient proof that the Pellmanns were indeed the happiest of parents.

Their friends often spoke of them in glowing terms. "They're the ideal couple," they said, but they did not see the truth—that the Pellmanns knew neither happiness nor fulfillment.

Heintz had been baptized in the Lutheran church and considered himself a Christian. But what a distant God he worshiped! He says, "I considered God to be no more than a higher power over the universe. I did not believe he was personally concerned with me. After all, I was just a tiny speck in that universe."

Back in Saxony, Mother Pellmann became his only connection with a life of faith. In her weekly letters she unfailingly asked God's blessing on her son's family. But instead life became more perplexing day by day, with a salary always too small, and nerves always jangled.

One morning Gertrude's sister appeared with rare good news. "Canada has opened the gates to German immigrants," she said. "Who wants to go?" Their minds lighted with thoughts of escape from their gloomy, crowded city life. Canada was limitless, with bright-faced people and oil wells and cattle and land. Surely, the ancient formula of hard work and long hours would make them rich and happy in the New World.

"We're going," Heintz and Gertrude decided.

In June of 1953 they arrived in Toronto. Their total capital was thirty borrowed dollars.

"What can you do?" employers asked, when he applied for a job.

"I can cook. I'm a chef," he replied, but as he spoke in German only, they sent him away.

Menial, temporary jobs kept them alive. "We worked hard for little money," he says, "but we did not mind because our hope was set on a prosperous future."

After a while, they sent for Gertrude's mother, and her 10-year-old brother. Now, they both could work, while mother cared for the family. After a while each of them won better jobs, and new friends. He really was a fine chef, and she was a capable and striking blonde beauty. Toronto's brilliant new skyscrapers reminded Heintz of great fortunes others had made. He walked down Bay Street past the Stock Exchange, the money hub of Canada, dreaming. On the north side of town, he saw the gigantic Norman castle called Casa Loma, 98 rooms which cost $3,000,000, with a stable that had solid mahogany stalls, erected by a local stockbroker. It was a monument to what one man could do. The city's slogan gave Heintz clear guidance. It read: "Industry, intelligence, integrity."

Yet, all the time the imp of insecurity gnawed at his vitals. He kept pressing, kept reaching out, never content. "We must own our own home," he told himself. "It'll help us to get ahead." He watched Gertrude's womanhood blossom as she learned Canadian ways, dressing better and speaking brightly. Good, he thought, she can

128

help me, too. He began to urge her to wear only the smartest dresses, to be what all the young women of this new city seemed to want to be: in fact, a glamor girl. Back home, they had been an ideal couple, now they became glamorous, and her beauty attracted many glances.

He bought his dream house, with roses climbing up one wall and a fenced-in play yard for the children. It should have multiplied his happiness, but it did not. He met acquaintances on the street and heard their praise of his achievements. When special events were scheduled in a downtown restaurant, he was often chosen to run the kitchen. These achievements only left him dissatisfied and empty.

"What a success story," friends said. "What a home, what a family, what a wife!"

What a wife, indeed, he thought bitterly, and before he knew or understood it, a big green bubble of jealousy had exploded inside him and turned everything to rubbish. "Things should have been rosy," he says. "We had liberty, success, a high living standard, and three sweet little girls had been added to our family. But my insecurity had grown. All of a sudden, it burst forth like a volcano. I began to mistrust my wife. In fact, I didn't trust anyone. It got worse and worse and I had no way to control it. Our family life was miserable, a horrible nightmare."

He went to a psychiatrist who recognized his mental illness and told him, "You're simply imagining things." Heintz stormed out of his office, unconvinced.

In truth, his life was falling apart because of a flaw he could not discern. In Germany, their first years together had brought unhappiness and a yearning to escape

129

from Europe. Now, with success and freedom, disaster was striking again. He came home one day and found his wife praying for him.

He was astonished that she should turn to God. Maybe it was a good idea for her, but certainly it was not for him. Two years earlier, a friend had given him a Bible, and he had handed it carelessly to her. In her great need, she had begun to read it.

"You ought to read it, too," she had told him.

"Why? I know all I need to know about the Bible."

From that day onward, Gertrude read the Bible daily. A Christian friend counseled her, leading her through the mystery of rebirth in the Holy Spirit. Each Sunday, she dressed her five children and took them to Sunday school and church.

Heintz reluctantly accompanied her. Some twinge of conscience, coming out of his childhood perhaps, told him that his salvation might be found in God's house, and now he wanted salvation desperately. So they walked into the sanctuary Sunday after Sunday. Neighborly tongues clucked busily at what a change had come over him; and they were half right. The outside was changed; he was resolved to become a good Christian, and to live righteously. He listened attentively to sermon after sermon. "Do this! . . . Don't do that!" . . . He grew dizzy.

"Nobody told me how to live right," he recalls.

And inside, in the part that nobody saw but himself, he was boiling with anger and suspicion. A devil inside prodded him endlessly. One day, he went to a detective agency, gave his wife's name and description, and said, "Watch her. Tell me everything she does, every person she talks to, everywhere she goes."

Now, he could rarely sleep. He never took time for his children. "I thought of myself as the provider," he says. "I'd play with the kids once in a while but most of the time I sat watching TV."

The detective agency observed every move Gertrude made. "She is blameless," they reported, "and entirely free from suspicion." Now he mistrusted the detectives.

Clearly, Heintz needed medical help, and it came through a nerve specialist who talked him into going into a hospital. Two weeks on his back, sedated, alone, gave him thinking time. One thing seemed very clear. His wife was finding much comfort in her Christian commitment; indeed, some of it seemed to rub off on him during her hospital visits.

In two weeks he was released, not healed but on the mend. Again, they went to church together. "It pleased me much to see her singing in the choir," he says. "After that first Sunday, I tried hard to live the Christian life in my own strength. But I didn't know how. What a frustrating experience! I didn't even read the Bible because I feared that Bible-reading might confuse one who has no theological training."

One Tuesday night, the phone rang. Heintz remembers the exact moment: "Our neighbors called us to their home to watch the Billy Graham crusade in Philadelphia on their TV. I was reluctant to go but I wanted to be a good neighbor, so I went.

"George Beverly Shea was singing beautifully—I liked it—and Billy preached, but I was immediately suspicious that he was trying to butter up the audience for something or other. Hearing his sermon, I thought, 'Yes, the world needs a man with a message like that. Yes, it's good for people.' " But he was thinking of others, not of himself.

On the second night, the neighbors called again. The jammed auditorium astonished Pellmann, bringing wonder that so many persons could be interested in religion. The huge choir sang a stirring hymn and then Beverly Shea came to the microphone. As his voice poured into that little sitting room, Heintz told himself, "It's like a prayer." Deeply moved, his eyes found the huge, lettered verse of Scripture over the pulpit, "I am the Way, the Truth and the Life." It was new to him and he wondered if it were really Scriptural.

Presently, Billy Graham explained many things, but two thoughts lodged in Heintz' mind. First, unless a man be born again, he cannot see the Kingdom of God. Second, salvation is a free gift of God, and all that a person has to do is to believe it.

"I thought I had to work at it to be a Christian," he says. He could hardly believe that Graham's teachings came from the Bible.

That next day, Gertrude noticed that he was gentler with her, and seemed almost eager to listen to the third telecast. Her prayers, full of love and winged by faith, never ceased. After dinner they sat down soberly with their neighbors and listened.

Again, Heintz heard a new message. "Mr. Graham was telling me not to clean up my life, but to come to Jesus just as I was, as a sinner, for Jesus' blood cleanses us from all sins. When the invitation was given, and "Just As I Am" was sung, the scales fell off my eyes and, in the very essence of the word, light flooded my soul. I was overjoyed

132

and felt as light as a feather. Suddenly, I realized I trusted the Savior completely, with my heart and soul, and my burden of sin was lifted, my conscience at peace."

By now, the Pellmanns were no longer in their chairs. They were on their knees. "For the first time in my life, I could pray from my heart," Heintz says. "I had never been able to pray except the Lord's prayer, or my childhood bedtime prayer, yet here I was on my knees in my neighbor's living room, asking the Lord to forgive my sins and cleanse my heart and fill me with his Holy Spirit."

Presently, he went back to his church, recharged, renewed, and outspoken. Wherever he went, he told people of the salvation he had found, of his escape from a living hell of unjustified tension and suspicion. The congregation rejoiced and soon elected him an elder. Some cautious souls warned his wife that he ought to tone down his tale of being reborn, while some even called him "the Bible-banger" and "Holy Joe." But he could not contain his delight. He and Gertrude prayed together for guidance, searched the Scriptures, and visited with other congregations. After a while, they settled down with a group of believers whose fellowship added to their conviction and their joy. They are still worshiping in that devoted band.

It is a fact that a Christian's status is rarely secure, and sometimes it consists of falling and being lifted up and falling and being lifted up again. But to recognize one's mistakes is perhaps the beginning of righteousness.

Heintz remembers, "My moral failure was to make my wife into a glamor girl, and to put far too much emphasis on beauty and sex in my married life. It was nothing less than idolatry."

Not long ago, someone asked him, "As a result of your decision, what differences did you notice?"

"I was a new person in Christ," he answered. "My heart was filled with love for all the world. My former race prejudice melted away. For the first time I thanked God for my wife and my children. I felt relief and joy, I felt clean inside. I had the assurance that I had finally found the truth."

Gertrude Pellmann, after her many times of trial, surely deserves the last word in this story. Secure in faith at last, she puts her joy this way: "Indeed, I have a new husband and the children have a new father. What a blessing for a couple to be not only of one flesh but also of one spirit. Praise the Lord."

Carry a Bible in your glove compartment

BIGGEST IN THE BUSINESS, HARDEST DRIVING, LONGEST WORKING, HE COULD NEVER FIND REAL SUCCESS UNTIL HE TURNED HIS AUTO BUSINESS OVER TO GOD.

John Hedges was headed for bankruptcy, if you believed the talk around town. The most successful auto dealer in the midwest, he had been living high on the hog for some years, throwing cocktail and poker parties in his luxurious summer place at Lake Wawasee, and in his winter apartment in Florida. His wife Wilma wore diamonds and furs, but close observers saw her worried eyes. As for John, he was big and hearty, as able a self-made man as you could find, but with a growing weakness for strong liquor. He drank for what he thought was a good reason.

"I got caught in a squeeze and in two years I lost nearly a half-million dollars," Hedges says. "Then the drink habit really began to take hold."

How he struggled back to a new life of self-respect and service to others is one of the great stories of today's business world.

He was born in a town called Paris Crossing, with a population of 132. His father was a tenant farmer. When he was 13 years old, a country preacher baptized him. It was the only contact he would have with God for years. Later, when he had become a hulking and muscular youth of 17, he quit school and took off. That was 1920, in the midst of the depression that followed World War I.

For a while he knew days of grinding labor. "I got a job on a 600-acre farm, rising at 5 a.m. and snapping eight tons of sweet corn per day for the cannery. They paid me a dollar a ton."

Next, he wandered to the nearest big city, Indianapolis, and got a job in the building trade. With too much energy to be satisfied with paid work, he soon opened a gravel pit and began to make and sell cement blocks.

Each morning a 15-year-old girl, on her way to school, walked along the railroad tracks next to the pit. Young Hedges watched her, deeply smitten. One day, he stopped at a friend's house to get water for his tractor and there met the distant beauty he worshiped. Blonde and willowy, her name was Wilma, and she was everything he had dreamed about. Soon, he stumbled through a proposal. Two years after meeting her, they were married.

Both of them wanted children. In 1928, Betty Lou was born, and then Charles in 1930. The babies arrived along with the greatest depression of the century. John was forced to shut down his business and go to work shoveling coal seven days a week for 50 cents a ton.

But he still had time to dream. He says, "I was like a lot of other Americans, determined to get to the top and become an operator. Why? Because I wanted things . . . a mink stole for Wilma, a grand piano in the library,

138

a grandfather clock, a plate rail in the dining room loaded with Haviland china."

When business picked up, he found a job selling cars and started to work his way up. The hours were long and he had no time for God. The church meant little to him.

One day in 1945, with the end of World War II in sight, when any car was certain to find a ready buyer following the wartime famine, Dame Fortune finally hit him over the head with her fairy wand. He had been a general sales manager for a big Chevrolet dealer. Now, he was offered the dealership for the famous Pontiac automobile. It would take cash, lots of it, but the opportunity was solid gold. He put his house on the market, borrowed where he could, and got the money together. Now he could "operate."

Not many men knew how to work as hard as John Hedges, and presently he outdistanced them all. It meant long hours and long Sundays at the showrooms, weariness, and taut nerves. It meant that he and Wilma were suddenly affluent, living better than had once seemed possible, but at a speed that was dizzying.

"I made up my mind that I would become one of the largest dealers in the state," he recalls. "And it came about."

Holidays were supposed to be relaxing. He remembers, "When we finally took a vacation, we drove I don't know how many thousands of miles in thirteen days, to California and Mexico, and back. I never worked so hard in my life."

One evening, he felt unusually low. A salesman said, "How about a drink? You'll feel better for it."

"I can sure use something."

He downed the liquor and the warmth spread through him, temporarily lifting his spirits. It was a step in the wrong direction. "Before long, we were serving cocktails at our parties. Then, the country club set began to accept us, so we went to their dances. And some of the folks with the most impressive connections in town began to include us in their guest lists. All at once, we were 'in,' and life was rich and lavish. If we weren't sleeping too well, what of it? Our agency was leading the whole world in Pontiac sales. I bought Wilma a diamond bracelet."

Imagine the distance they had come. Presently that country boy working a gravel pit and that willowy blonde who had walked the railroad track found themselves socializing with the town's big entertainers, following the sun south for the winter, and buying only the best for themselves and their children.

And then the squeeze came, the squeeze for which no human is ever adequately prepared. With five used-car lots, he was overextended, and for the first time, hard work would not turn the tide. Deeply concerned, unable to sleep, puzzled and plagued by fear, John and Wilma examined their lives and felt that something was radically wrong.

But what? Nobody could tell them, not at first.

Then came an unforgettable experience. John says, "I woke up one morning to find Wilma crying." She said, "John, I had a dream. In it, the Lord came and gave me a warning. He said, 'If you don't change your ways, worse things will happen.' "

John was speechless and stunned. Two weeks earlier, in a dream of his own, he, too, had seen the face of Jesus.

140

One night, their doorbell rang. Their caller was the Rev. Ozie Pruett, minister of the First Baptist Church. He was a friend, though not really close, and they had attended his church. Making his rounds, looking for lost sheep, he had come to ask the Hedges to think seriously about giving God a place in their lives. "Billy Graham is coming to hold a crusade here this October," he said. "I think you might want to hear what he has to say."

"Who," John asked, with some asperity, "is Billy Graham?"

Presently, he found out. First, he met Grady Wilson, a team member who led the crusade's advance guard. They played a round of golf together, and when Graham arrived for the crusade, he also took an afternoon off to join John Hedges on the fairways. When they parted, the evangelist challenged, "You and your wife come out to the fair grounds. We're having some glorious meetings."

"After that first night, Wilma came home and wept," Hedges remembers. "She said she wouldn't go back. Then she explained, 'I can't go back, unless I go forward.'"

"Graham's not talking to you," Hedges told her. "He's talking to real sinners." In his heart, he knew differently.

What happened next? The crusade was closing with a great meeting at the state fair racetrack. Hedges has retold the story joyously to clubs, conventions, friends, and school groups: "Wilma and I decided to go. When we reached the grandstand she asked me, 'What are you going to do?' I couldn't answer, so I just ignored her and listened to the choir rehearsing. I still remember that song. It was 'Deep down in my heart the love of Jesus is singing. . . .'"

And he goes on: "That afternoon, God reached down in mercy and picked both of us out of our hell. The man he sent began to talk and he just kept talking to my heart. When the invitation was given we both went forward, so nervous we could hardly stand still. Then we met our counselors and they started us on the Bible lessons; and do you know, we've been studying them ever since."

What of today? Does the powerful businessman still follow the narrow road? The words of John Hedges give answer: "The Lord sent us many Christian friends who had fellowship with us and helped us grow."

Their children, Betty Lou and Charles, though never taken once to Sunday school in their childhood, accepted the Lord and entered the church.

His auto business boomed. But not for Hedges' personal glory, as he is quick to point out. "I've made a deal with the Lord," he says. "It is now his business, not mine. I'm only running it for him."

Most important, the old life of fear and sleeplessness has turned to one of service and joy. A reporter once asked him what he does today that is different from the old days. His explanation was simple and uncomplicated; yes, he and Wilma read the Bible every day, starting right after an early dinner and lasting sometimes to eleven o'clock; no, he almost never turns on the TV or radio or reads a newspaper. On occasion, they play the phonograph so they can hear some of their records which explain passages of Scripture.

"We never miss church," he says. "We go to get our souls fed and to glorify the Lord."

Down in Florida one winter, they encountered old friends who were as deeply troubled as once the Hedges had been. "I like to do personal work," he says. "We led them to the Lord."

He has given his testimony in many of the high schools of Indianapolis and before dozens of business groups. Wilma also serves, working with needy children and the elderly. "The lavish spending has gone out of our lives," he reports, "but we've discovered the excitement of tithing for the Lord."

But one other thing makes John Hedges a unique business manager, arising from his awareness of an opportunity and his personal method of testifying. As an automobile dealer and soldier of Christ, he undertook a project back in 1959 which has since reached people from coast to coast, and which has crowded his files with letters of joyous, surprised gratitude. But let him tell about it.

He says, "Every new car or late-model used car that we sell is delivered to the customer with a New Testament in the glove compartment. By now, our service attendants have placed our Testaments in over seven thousand cars."

Can a businessman be a Christian and stay in business? John Hedges, one of the busiest and biggest of businessmen, makes this answer:

"I don't see how, in this day and age, any man can stay in business, and not be a Christian who takes Christ along with him. We all know that there is misrepresentation among some businessmen. But I've found that by trusting the Lord and letting him guide me, I have had no trouble whatsoever. He is really a wonderful Savior."

A physician learns his gods are false

AT HARRINGAY, HE STUDIED GRAHAM
WITH BINOCULARS AND CAMERA,
AND DISCOVERED A MEDICINE THAT
COULD HEAL THE WORLD.

"Do these converts last? After so many years, I consider that a very silly question." The professor of theology leaned back, grinning impishly.

His desk was piled high with books, records, typewritten sheets. In an open drawer I saw canceled airplane tickets and travel itineraries. For the past year, he had been tracking down men and women who were converted in various Billy Graham crusades. He snapped forward. "Who would you say is the person *least* likely to come forward at a crusade?"

"I'd say a journalist, or a man with a scientific background."

"Like a doctor, maybe?"

"Yes, a doctor's a scientist."

The theologian plunged into a deep drawer, burying his head and shoulders, and the only sound was the scraping of papers. "Ah!" He surfaced like a porpoise. "You ask for a doctor. I give you a doctor. Read." He thrust a sheaf of tablet paper into my hands. "He was a vile man, with an abased mind. A fine physician but with the prurient thoughts of a satyr."

The document in my hands was titled, "Testimony of Dr. David Rowlands." A kind of dun-colored foolscap, of indifferent quality, showed almost illegible typewriting. A careful hand had gone down the lines making corrections with a pencil.

"Anybody can write a good yarn," I said. "But the proof is living it. What do you really know about Rowlands?"

His hand shot forward. "Give it back! If you don't believe, if you cannot see the nose on your face, give it back!"

"Relax," I said. "But we both know plenty of fakers."

"Stop talking and read," he said.

I am a doctor with a Christian wife and six children, David Rowlands wrote. Formerly a skeptic, I came to a personal knowledge of Christ at Harringay in 1954 during the Billy Graham Greater London crusade. From that moment on I have never been the same man.

I already had position, a prosperous London practice, a lovely home and all the modern luxuries that money could buy. Yet I was still restless and discontented with life. Life seemed to be a never-ending search for peace of mind and happiness. I had been brought up by fine parents in a good Christian home and hence I had presumed I was a Christian, although I have to admit, church-going was mostly boring and time consuming. The Bible was just a history book and prayer was unreal.

God had spoken to me several times. He had saved me from the German bombing of Liverpool, from shipwreck, and after nine months of paralyzing illness had granted complete recovery; but I still hardened my heart toward Him.

Out of curiosity I went to hear Billy Graham. The message he preached was quite new to me. He kept repeating what God says in the Bible; I had been used to sermons based on rational arguments. I found his sermons heart-searching and disturbing, realizing for the first time in my life that I was a sinner, that my sins separated me from God: the sins of self, of lust, of materialism. These were my gods and the Bible teaches "Thou shalt have no other gods before me." I had broken the first commandment. I was a sinner needing a Savior.

Without Billy's challenge I should never have found the Savior and would still be searching. On my fifth attendance I made the decision through which God changed my whole life. I surrendered myself unreservedly to Christ. I had gone to the meetings armed with binoculars and camera but I did not come away with the picture of a man, but with the very real presence of Christ—the greatest proof of the resurrection any man could desire. I came face to face with the risen Christ. He means more to me now than anything else this world affords. What a privilege to know Him; what a responsibility to make Him known.

Little did I realize then all the wonder that was to follow. I seemed to enter a new world in a fourth dimension with Christ within me directing my thoughts, words, and actions. I came to experience a wonderful peace and joy. Life seemed to make sense at last.

The Bible became alive and I was hungry to read what God had to say to me in it. Unfortunately my church was spiritually cold and apathetic toward Billy Graham's work, but the crusade team's weekly follow-up classes were invaluable. Meeting my wife in a crowded thoroughfare, I gave her my news, and abandoning shyness, she expressed her exuberant joy by kissing and embracing me. She had been praying seven years for this moment.

Little did I realize where Christ could lead me. Besides carrying on my practice, I was to spend the next three years traveling in Britain, especially on weekends, giving my testimony and the vital Gospel message to churches of all denominations and to hospitals, and I was privileged to witness a wonderful harvest following in the wake of the crusade. It was a great honor also to give a brief testimony on the "Hour of Decision."

Soon after my conversion, one of my patients of another faith tried to commit suicide. After a week in which her life was in the balance, the hospital discharged her. She phoned me when she arrived home and asked for a tonic. The best medicine I knew was a dose of Billy Graham's preaching, so I took her to hear him. She accepted Christ and became a radiant Christian and has won two colleagues for the Lord.

Keen for my patients to hear Billy Graham, I organized six busloads and advertised new bus stops to pick up passengers on their way to Harringay. Hearing of it, the Ministry of Transport ordered me to cancel my plans as I had contravened some obscure part of the traffic act. However, after giving my testimony to several officials and

148

eventually to the VIP at the top, the committee broke their rule and allowed the buses to run. That day twelve more souls were saved.

After accepting Christ I could not reconcile my old taste in literature with my new experience, and anyway my appetite had changed. One night on my way home from Harringay, I threw my sensational literature and pinup calendars over London Bridge into the River Thames. A suspicious policeman rushed to inquire what the bundle contained and was very skeptical when I told him the truth.

After Harringay, my wife and I felt led to hold "Harringay" crusades in our own home. We did this fortnightly for three years. There were often fifty to sixty patients and friends present and there were a number of decisions. I also felt motivated to hold monthly Sunday film services in the local Civic Hall. This has now grown into a regular interdenominational youth crusade. I believe Christian films and cottage meetings are a real means of winning the outsider to Christ and his Church.

My patients came to know a new doctor, one who now did not mind what time the phone rang, one who was ready to listen to the stories of broken homes, to their worries, fears, and anxieties. My patients also discovered that the prescription they got was often different, too. In selected cases I would point them to Christ who alone can break the tension underlying a duodenal ulcer or nervous breakdown. I know from experience only God is big enough to fill the vacuum in the human soul, and mend the broken home.

My secretary, a worldly person with no church background, said to me one day, "You have changed so much; if it's something you got from Billy Graham, then I want it too." So I took her and her husband to the last night of the crusade. Both were converted and now hold cottage meetings of their own.

We joined a fine local church where God's word is faithfully preached and which has just inaugurated an all-age Sunday school.

Two years ago my wife and I and the six children emigrated to New Zealand, not knowing what the future would hold but relying on the promise that "when he pusheth forth his sheep he goeth before them."

I am still a doctor but have been privileged to speak at numerous Auckland churches and on the air, paving the way for Billy Graham's recent crusade here. The spiritual hunger at two youth camps at which I spoke recently can be judged by the fact that at each, over thirty young people made decisions for Christ.

The New Zealand Crusade was the greatest, Billy says, of any six days of his entire ministry. For me there were two highlights.

Firstly, the decisions of our two older children to accept Christ. The eldest already has her eye on the mission field.

Secondly, the thrilling visit of Billy Graham to our home in Auckland; a joy and privilege we shall always treasure, because of his warm Christian love and interest in our affairs. He had called to see how the Christian babe of 1954 was growing in the Lord. I hope he was not disappointed.

Knowing the pitfalls and needs of new converts, my wife and I are holding weekly follow-up classes in our

150

home for about 30 professional and business folk who made decisions for Christ at Billy Graham's Auckland crusade. We are glad to pass on the follow-up instructions received following the London crusade. The meetings here scheduled for one hour often extend to three hours, such is the hunger of the new converts.

"But why," I can hear you say, "do you spend all your spare time on evangelism?" If you had discovered that the secret of life is in Christ you'd want to share Him too. If you saw your friend drowning you'd want to save him too. And having wasted thirty-five years I want to make up for them, in full measure.

Do crusade converts last? Billy Graham was converted when he was a teenager attending a tabernacle revival. Telling of his conversion, he once said, "I have lasted. Cliff Barrows has lasted. Colleen Townsend, a former movie starlet, has lasted. I know hundreds of factory workers, business executives, and professional people who have lasted.

"After Harringay, the *Reader's Digest* picked a hundred names at random of people who made decisions in London. And you know, they found only *one* person who said he didn't mean it."

Conversion: A first person confession

THE TESTIMONY OF A YOUNG CHURCH ORGANIST WHO THOUGHT HE WAS SMARTER THAN GOD.

Subject: TESTIMONY OF A SAVING ADVENTURE

To: THE BILLY GRAHAM EVANGELISTIC
ASSOCIATION

From: WESLEY H. DICKENS

I heard the minister say, "Don't drink! Don't smoke! Don't swear!" But those suggestions left my youthful questions unanswered. Who is Christ? How can I love God? How can a man be saved? I wanted to know.

Presently, I found that I no longer cared who Christ was. I thought perhaps I didn't need to be saved. Religion became just a Sunday exercise. In fact, loving God seemed like a pretty silly idea.

The effect of these notions on my living was disastrous. I was resentful, discourteous, disobedient to my parents, hateful, intemperate, even blasphemous. Yet through it all, I never missed a single Sunday service. I was there in the pew with a thick veneer of morality and refinement upon my person. Not because I liked it, but because my parents insisted on it. Unlike some parents, they even went to church themselves. But I hated the services, the long-winded prayers, the mediocre choir, the boring sermons.

The beginning of the long hard pull to God began when I entered Westminster Choir College in Princeton, New Jersey, to study church music. It was not that I wanted to work in the church, but I played the pipe organ and felt that music was my only talent.

In my first year, I began to visit the local Episcopal church. Soon, I came to think that the Episcopal Church had all the answers. I learned about the Trinity, the Virgin Birth, the Atonement, the Resurrection, and the Second Coming. I also studied church history, the prayer book, the Sacraments, the Bible, and the lives of the saints. I came to feel that any person who was not an Episcopalian was a heretic.

In consequence, I forsook the Methodism of my childhood and was confirmed by the Bishop. I had been taught that by the imposition of the Bishop's hands, I would happily receive the Holy Ghost. Not in my case. Instead, after my Confirmation, I became increasingly afraid of the Holy Ghost.

In June of 1956, I left Westminster Choir College and returned to my home in New Jersey. I wasted no love on my mother and brother. My father's death taught me nothing. Finally, I behaved so abominably that my mother evicted me, and I went to live at the YMCA in the city of Paterson.

There at the Y, at night, in the darkness and quiet of my room, my fear of the Holy Ghost mounted until it quite obsessed me. In bed, I saw constantly in my mind's eye a grisly Angel of Doom coming through the darkened

154

window to snatch me away to hell. I became panic-stricken as I imagined the footsteps of the Holy Ghost approaching. Sometimes I could hear the sound of His "breathing" and could feel His "wind." I was convinced at these times that He was close by. Praying made matters worse. Sometimes I rushed to the nearest telephone to call my pastor. More often I was so paralyzed with fear that I could not move.

One day my fear disappeared very suddenly, because I seemed to have lost my religion. I looked up to heaven, saying, "Do you exist, O God?" But now I suffered more acutely than before, for when I had feared God, I had at least believed that He existed.

I sat down at my desk with paper and pencil in hand. "I'm going to prove the Christian religion," I said. It took me three months, but, step by step, my faith returned, whole and complete, proved scientifically and mathematically on paper. But that was just the trouble. The religion that I had proved true was worth about as much to me as the paper upon which my arguments were written. Christianity meant no more to me than the knowledge that two and two makes four. My empty orthodoxy harassed me until May 1957, when Billy Graham came to New York City.

Early in May, the Bishop Coadjutor of Newark sent out a letter to all the clergy. From many an Anglican pulpit the letter was read, urging the support of the Billy Graham New York crusade.

At the little mission of the Epiphany, in Allendale, the Rev. Johann Schenk read the letter, then added a few words of his own. Father Schenk set to work getting groups together to attend the crusade meetings at Madison Square Garden in New York City. One night, quite out of curiosity, I went along.

I heard Billy Graham preach the Gospel that night, and suddenly I knew that I was not a Christian. At the end of the sermon came an altar call. This was the time to give myself to Jesus Christ. The preacher said, "Come!" The choir began to sing. Suddenly the Garden became a great cathedral.

A yearning filled my heart; I wanted to give myself. As the choir sang its heavenly music, hundreds were streaming down the aisles of the great building in silent reverence, and a good-sized crowd was forming in front of the speaker's platform. People stood with heads upraised, as if awaiting a gift. My heart groaned and I felt a strong pull upon me, as if from a great magnet, which almost lifted me out of my seat.

"I can't go," I thought. "Father Schenk thinks I'm already converted. He knows that I want to be a priest. I'll make a fool of myself."

That wasn't the last meeting that I attended. Two weeks later I brought my two best friends with me. When the altar call was given, I felt the same reaction, only it was more intense. I could hardly keep my seat. I made a compromise. "If my friends go forward, I'll go." They looked as if they were hypnotized, staring ahead at the evangelist, as though enchanted.

As we started to leave the arena, my friends turned on me. "Why didn't you get up?" said Tom, almost savagely. "We were waiting for you."

Before we left Madison Square Garden, we made a pact: we would return and give our lives to Jesus Christ.

156

On Saturday evening, June 22, Tom and I were back. George was not with us. As the choir began to sing at the end of the service, Tom tugged at my sleeve. "I'm scared," he said. "I don't think I can do it."

I said, "I'll be with you."

On the second verse of the hymn I tapped Tom on the arm. "Let's go."

The walk to the platform at Madison Square Garden was the longest I have ever taken. When we finally arrived, we found ourselves in a crowd of hundreds. Some knelt. Some wept. Others turned their faces toward the evangelist as though he were the source of Light. Billy Graham looked down at me, or so I thought, for I had been introduced to him a few weeks before. I dropped my eyes to the floor. I already had an idea of what I was going to do.

Tom and I were overtaken by counselors who took us to a room downstairs. When we were seated, I leaned toward my counselor and whispered in his ear. "You needn't bother, I'm already a Christian. I'm only here to give my friend moral support."

"Are you sure?" he asked.

"Sure, I'm sure!"

When I returned to my room at the YMCA that night, I felt like kicking myself around the block for passing up such a golden opportunity to receive Christ. But I was convinced I'd put one over on Tom. I should have known better.

The next three weeks were hell. Every night I fell down at a little homemade altar I had built and tried to say a prayer to Jesus Christ, asking Him to make me a Christian. But it never worked. A passage of Scripture kept running through my mind: "Whosoever shall not confess Me before men, him will I deny before My Father which is in heaven."

During those three weeks other conversions occurred in our church with me in the supporting role. Each time I walked up that aisle—first with Tom, then with Ruth, and later with George—I felt that somehow I was really going up for myself, but I could never bring myself to tell anybody about it. My answer to the counselors was always the same: "I am already a Christian."

Saturday night, July 13, 1957, is a night I shall never forget.

"One thing thou lackest!" The evangelist's voice boomed, and reverberated a thousand times in my heart. "One thing thou lackest!" We were sitting in the balcony, three girls and myself. It was my fifteenth crusade meeting.

"Now, come," said the preacher, pleading. The choir began to sing.

> "Just as I am, without one plea,
> But that Thy blood was shed for me,
> And that Thou bidd'st me come to Thee,
> O Lamb of God, I come—I come."

More than ever before, I wanted to go up front with the many hundreds that were responding. "Come on, we're going to wait on you."

I turned to the girls beside me. "Don't any of you want to go up?"

"No!"

"Well," I thought, "if I go up without the girls, one of two things will happen. Either they'll follow me against their will, or we'll miss our bus and their parents will be on my neck for keeping them out to all hours. Besides, I can come alone tomorrow night and give my life to Christ then. Of course, Father Schenk will be notified, but that can't be helped. Yes, I'll come back tomorrow night." Thus Satan reasoned with my heart.

After a time, the choir stopped singing. "Thank God," I said, but I was not really relieved. "Well, it's too late now. It's got to be tomorrow night. There's no choice." I settled back in my seat. But I could not relax. The text of the sermon kept hounding me: "One thing thou lackest! One thing thou lackest!"

"Wait! I'm sorry, but there's something I must do." Billy Graham had moved to the microphone once more. "I've never done this before in the whole crusade, but I won't feel at peace tonight unless I do it. I have the feeling that there is *one* person out in the audience who ought to be up here!"

I wasn't prepared for this.

"That person needs Christ tonight. He's gripping his seat to keep from coming." There was a dreadful silence. I looked down at my hands. They were clamped so tightly around the chair that my knuckles were white. I let go so suddenly that I nearly slid onto the floor.

Billy Graham's voice rose with sudden excitement. "I think it's a young man—out *there*—in the balcony!" He thrust his hand in my direction. I began to sweat. Then I began to shake.

"He thinks he can come another night." There was a pause. He pointed his forefinger up into the balcony at me, and with all his power he said, "I want to tell you something, young man, whoever you are! You can't come

159

to Christ any time you want to! You can come only when the Spirit of God is drawing you! Now," he said more quietly, "I'm going to ask the choir to sing one verse of 'Almost Persuaded' while you come."

> "Almost persuaded, now to believe,
> Almost persuaded, Christ to receive."

That was all I could take. Turning to the girls, I cried in desperation, "Don't any of you want to go forward? There's still time." They shook their heads with terrible finality. "Well, then," I hardly knew I said it, "you'll have to excuse me, because I've got to." I turned my face abruptly away and leaped out of my seat. With head swimming and knees shaking, I made it to the escalator and then downstairs. Not another person was moving in the great building as I ran towards the rostrum. Thousands of people were on every side, but I no longer cared. In fact, now I wanted the whole world to see. As I ran, I almost cried aloud: "I'm coming, Lord Christ!"

And so I returned to my room that night, stunned by it all, knowing one thing only: I was saved. Yes, *saved*, right here and now, and forever!

I went to my church the next day and told all the people what the Lord had done.

"How do you account for it?" I said to Tom's mother.

"I'll try to explain," she said. "Tom knew what you did that night."

"I thought I'd pulled the wool over his eyes."

"Well, you hadn't. He came home and said, 'I guess because Wesley is going to be a priest he thinks he doesn't need to be converted, but he's wrong.' " She looked at me in silence for a moment. "He's been praying for you, Wesley."

While I yet tried to fathom the meaning of these words, I went to George and told him about our friend Tom. "Did you know that this was going on?" I asked.

"Yes," he said.

"But my experience in the Garden, George, how did that happen?"

"All of us have been praying for you," he said.

NOTE: Late in 1966—nine years later—the author talked to Rev. Johann Schenk, formerly pastor of the Church of the Epiphany in Allendale, N.J., for whose congregation young Wesley Dickens had played the organ. "He is now organist for the Church of the Atonement in Fair Lawn, N.J.," the Reverend Schenk said, "and he is a most consecrated and constant Christian. I think his conversion has definitely stayed within him and he has become a remarkably well-rounded personality. Indeed, he is a very brilliant person. He will tell you, I'm sure, that his conversion experience has had a lasting effect on him."

"My life was a mess."

A RESEARCHER, DEACON AND COLLEGE
PROFESSOR, HE TRIED THE INTELLEC-
TUAL APPROACH TO GOD—IN VAIN!
AND THEN A YOUTH RALLY SHOWED
THE WAY.

A scientist likes to have things in order, with facts that are proven and theories that are predictable. When Dr. Fred Smith, prize-winning biochemist of the University of Minnesota, first looked at the Kingdom of God, and then examined his personal relationship to it, he hoped to find an orderly, inevitable scientific arrangement.

He says, "My life was a mess."

Unaccountably, science had failed to iron out the wrinkles of his troubled soul. The skills that he had perfected in working at Oak Ridge on the atomic bomb and which had won him the Hudson Award and caused him to be named biochemist of the year, had neither given his mind peace nor his soul the knowledge of salvation.

A surprising invitation came one day, to attend a rally organized by a group of young evangelists in Minneapolis, called Youth for Christ.

163

"The speaker is Billy Graham," they said.

"Billy Graham, that preacher who talks a mile a minute on radio?"

"That's the man."

"He's a psychological misfit," Smith said. "I can't stand his stuff."

"He's part of your world. Don't you want to understand your world?"

So Dr. Fred Smith attended a 1957 youth rally in Minneapolis. It was one of the first steps he had ever taken outside the realm of his scientific universe.

Those young people talked much about God at their rally. But what is God to a scientist? "I never heard about such a creature," he says, recalling his own youth. "I don't remember ever hearing about God."

Smith was a young British intellectual. At the University of Birmingham, he had spent countless hours in the laboratory probing the complexities of the chemical structure of the carbohydrate molecules called polysaccharides. In succession, he earned doctorates in science and philosophy. When he thought beyond his field to human problems, he opined they might all be solved if only enough intellectuals got together and organized a thoughtful, scientific plan.

"I believed with my whole heart that this was the right answer," he recalls. "Surely, all the problems of the world could thus be solved, including our personal ones."

When the British government assigned him to Oak Ridge during World War II, he met and married a young Lutheran social worker. Three years later, he was appointed professor of biochemistry at the University of Minnesota.

164

Presently he became famous and respected and comfortable. America, the land of plenty, was as generous to him as to any of its native sons. Children were born, a fine home was bought, along with a car, TV set, washing machine, club memberships, credit cards; as they say, "the whole bit."

Describing his religious life, he says, "I was a deacon in the church, my wife and children attended services regularly, but it was mostly a Sunday performance. Apart from the meetings we attended together, I never got involved."

But his questing brain soon perceived an omission in his ordered life. "I knew that my intellectual approach to everything was not sufficient. I knew it was not producing answers to satisfy the problems of my own life; and I could see that it was not providing answers in the lives of other people."

When he joined the throngs of young people at that youth rally in 1957, his initial attitude was one of supercilious amusement. As the meeting moved along, giving time to what any sophisticate would call "cornball" antics, he felt vastly removed and superior. This feeling was shared by most of the others in his party, a group assembled by his pastor to attend the rally and hear the young evangelist named Graham.

Smith felt as smug and full of rectitude as any Sadducee, because, as he admits, "I found it very difficult to find in myself any of the world's enormous sins. Not until I became a Christian did I fully realize that I was a sinner!"

In some Christians, conversion is not instantaneous, but rather a growth process. For Fred Smith, it started

165

when he was middle-aged and aware finally that his great love called science had narrow limitations.

So the service and its juvenile interludes progressed to its climax and Billy Graham rose to preach. At once the picture began to change. Graham's manner was so full of confidence and so bold in his love of God that Professor Smith felt envy. Presently, he was sitting on the edge of his seat, living through what was, for him, his first encounter with Jesus.

Graham had begun to tell the story of Nicodemus, the powerful Pharisee and member of the Jerusalem Sanhedrin. Troubled and truth seeking, he had come secretly to Jesus. Climbing unseen up the outside stairway to the roof of the home where Jesus rested, he had slipped into the guest chamber.

"How like a scientist," Smith thought. "How typical of the attitude of the intellectually curious man. He will never take an open stand on any issue. He will go by night so that his professorial colleagues will not know what he's looking for."

Jesus dealt candidly with his distinguished visitor. Quickly he explained, unless you are born again, you cannot see the Kingdom of Heaven. Nicodemus wondered, how does a grown man manage to be born again? Knowing the scientific answer, he argued: Does one enter his mother's womb a second time to be born again?

Jesus would not be trapped, replying with a spiritual explanation. Again, the Pharisee pressed him. "But how can these things be?"

Jesus said, "Art thou a master of Israel, and knowest not these things?" His explanation had presented earthly matters, and Nicodemus had not believed him. If he were

166

to talk about heavenly matters, would the Pharisee believe him?

Jesus said, "As Moses lifted up the serpent in the wilderness, so must the Son of Man be lifted up, that whoever believes in him may have eternal life. For God so loved the world that he gave his only Son, that whoever believes in him should not perish but have eternal life."

The Pharisee was about to withdraw, when Jesus laid this personal charge on him, saying: "And this is the judgment, that the light has come into the world, and men loved darkness rather than light because their deeds were evil. For everyone who does evil hates the light and does not come into the light lest his deeds should be exposed. But he who does what is true comes to the light, that it may be clearly seen that his deeds have been wrought by God."

Doctor Smith recalls, "While Graham preached I became completely identified with this person Nicodemus. All of a sudden, it seemed, my search for reality had entered a new phase. I knew I was about to embark on the greatest experiment of all. I knew I would have to be 'born again.' "

Like Nicodemus, he did not yet understand how this was to be. He knew it was impossible biologically and in every other scientific way, and he knew that Jesus had dismissed the matter with the injunction to Nicodemus: "Marvel not that I said unto thee, Ye must be born again."

Presently, Graham gave the invitation, and hundreds of young men and women responded. Fred Smith and his wife and their party did not stir. His mind was still trying to figure things out. "It is typical of all intellectuals that we want everything brought under logical control," he said much later. "But it doesn't work out that way. The mystery of God is involved."

The service ended and they returned to their car to commence the long drive home. Now the evening began to make a new kind of sense. Clearly, a man had to choose between light and darkness. While the others talked, he was silent.

"Just when I received Jesus Christ personally, I'm not sure," he recalls. "We were riding home from the rally and I heard a lady who was with us say something that probably clinched the issue. She said, 'Well, we don't go for this emotional business. We prefer the intellectual approach.'

"While she was speaking, I think I took a really big jump. She didn't know I had been trying to make the intellectual approach to reality for years and had found it completely inadequate."

That jump, however, was not the total surrender that Christ demands. But it led his thoughts to areas of truth he had never previously accepted.

"The next few days were strange, indeed," he says. "I spent my off hours walking around in my garden, puzzling over Billy Graham's words and reading the Bible. From time to time, I was startled to find myself gripped by intense feelings of such great joy that I wept. At the moment, I was not even aware of this, and my wife pointed it out to me later.

"While it was unclear to me what was happening, I think God must have intervened at precisely that time. The whole experience was crystallized one morning while I was on my way to the university to give my usual lecture. As I drove through one of our beautiful parks, it was

168

brought home to me that this Jesus was the standard for which I was looking. He was the standard of reference for my whole life."

As this change took place in Doctor Smith's mind and heart, he came to understand the meaning of Christ's death on the Cross, and the true meaning of sin. "It really isn't difficult to discover the enormity of one's sins," he says. "You come upon this knowledge very fast. The nature of sin is quite different from what many people think. It is not so much what we do as what we are."

As his regeneration continued, gradually but inexorably, other things became clear. "I experienced peace of mind and freedom from fear," he says. "We cold scientists like to put a veneer on our behavior, and to keep our feelings and fears subdued, but they are always with us. As I began to acquire a greater understanding of the Bible, my growth in the Christian life brought the release of tension and the stability and joy that Jesus Christ alone provides."

He made another important discovery. "After I came to the conclusion that Jesus is the Christ, I realized that, as a scientist, I had been living a fantastic life of faith. We do many experiments on faith. We accept much information on faith. Scientists believe in electrons and protons and other atomic particles, yet nobody has ever seen such a particle. We have faith that the textbooks describing these things are true, yet we know very well that these textbooks are being changed and modified so constantly that only the newest book is relevant to modern scientific activity. And yet, incredibly, we often dismiss the Bible which has remained virtually unchanged for almost two thousand years."

169

In the excitement of his new understanding of the Gospel, Doctor Smith began to invite people to his home for discussion and prayer. After a while, a regular weekly meeting night was named to which neighbors and visitors rallied in increasing numbers. Discussions were frank and direct, avoiding theological riddles but emphasizing the claim of Christ upon human lives. Most of Fred Smith's visitors had never heard those claims before. Like him, many of them were seeking and hungry.

As the last act of this living drama unfolded, Fred Smith's living room became a small sanctuary and his discourses provided a blueprint for the salvation that awaited men. During a single year, as one modern Nicodemus after another visited his home and revealed his need in prayer and study, forty-two of them were led into the spiritual kingdom of Christ.

The end of the great quest

SHE WAS SICK OF LUKEWARM RELI-GION. WHEN THE TV VOICE SAID "COME!" SHE FELL ON HER KNEES, SAY-ING, "WHAT WILL YOU HAVE ME DO?"

Mabel Duvall would like to call this story "The End of The Great Quest."

As she lived it, she often wondered if she would ever see its ending. But she did, and the manner of her survival charted a course that others can follow. Like many another private journey, it began in misery and self-doubt in the home of well-meaning parents.

Her personal history shows that she asked for full membership in a solid Methodist church at the age of nine. All her young friends were doing the same thing, most of them simply following the urge to conform, and she had no idea of the gravity of her step. "I knew nothing of a personal relationship with Christ," she says. "To me, Jesus was simply a wonderful person who lived in Bible stories and Sunday-school lessons much as George Washington lived in my history books."

So she was admitted to membership, the months lengthened into years, and the security she sought was lost under a mounting tide of unease. Finally, an evangelist came to her church, preaching about a personal Savior, and she responded to his words. "Gladly I walked down the aisle," she says.

The pride and joy she took from that selfless act had not long to live. "My parents," she recalls, "were horrified that I had done such a strange thing." Each dinnertime, they pressed her with questions. Was she not already a church member? Had somebody used undue influence on her? And, besides, how could such a young miss know enough about sin to want to be forgiven? "I was made to feel that I had shamed and disgraced my parents before the whole town," she says.

She revealed her humiliation to no one, not wishing to court further ridicule, and she joined the army of "Sunday Christians." On Sundays, she was always in church, but her mind and her interests were far away. As a girl, she had sung Gospel hymns and memorized Bible verses, but these commendable habits ebbed and stopped. Such a sense of futility replaced her old buoyancy that she finally cried, "Dear God, why did you ever let me be born?"

With each passing year, she tried to fill her days with more books, more music, and more work. Since she was young, popular, and sought after, a golden vista of tomorrows beckoned, and she danced into young womanhood with most of her unanswered questions pushed out of her mind.

"Before old age, I'll surely find the solution to

everything," she reckoned. "Yes, and also to the right relationship with God."

Only occasionally, she would hear a soft warning, "But what if you should die today?"

At college, she competed earnestly for the Bible medal, not as an application of Christ's teaching but as a memory exercise. Soon she had graduated and gone to work in the nation's capital city. Now, away from home, she could do exactly as she pleased. She no longer had any reason to attend church.

The man she met presently became her husband, and a new and thrilling chapter began. She established her own home, went to school and got a degree, and started a career as a government servant. It was exciting, it was Godless, and so it remained for eight years.

She looks back, wonderingly. "Was my conscience asleep? I had uncomfortable moments, a feeling of missing something important. And I'd hear a voice that said, 'If you were to die today, would you be ready to meet God?' "

So the quest, the great quest about which she would learn much later, began with timid, tentative visits to several churches. Finally, a decision was made, and she joined an Episcopal church. After some Bible study, she went to the usual confirmation service. "As I bowed my head in its white veil before a candlelit altar," she recalls, "the bishop performed the ancient rite of the laying on of hands, and I took solemn vows to follow Jesus Christ as my Lord and Savior."

"At last, I have come home," she mused. "Now I'll have peace and the assurance of salvation."

So she followed her church's ritual earnestly, singing its hymns, kneeling in prayer, reverently partaking of communion. But distress invaded her mind and grew like a thundercloud. "Something important is missing," she thought. But what was it?

Her life began to drift once more, separating her from God's church because no guide stood near to counsel her, to reveal either the depth of her needs or God's graciousness and love. So her heart and mind built defenses against hurt, and she went her way, desperately hoping that nothing would disturb her little world.

It seemed safe and sane enough until one shattering summer morning when she was summoned to her office phone.

"Mrs. Duvall," the voice said, "your husband has collapsed at work. He's been rushed to the hospital."

"Is he all right?"

"You'd better get there right away."

She sped to the hospital, filled with panic as never before in her life. He had been so strong, so ever present. The thought of his death turned in her mind like a crooked blade.

"Dear God, save him," she begged. "Give him back to me and I'll serve you forever."

At the hospital, they told an amazing tale. "Her husband was pronounced dead on arrival at a doctor's office," they explained, "but adrenaline injections were given routinely. And suddenly, his heart began to beat again."

"It's a miracle," she said. "Thank you, Father."

Within weeks, such is the inconstancy of the well-fed conscience, she had forgotten her promise. Whenever it spoke, she side-stepped its demands. "I was still trying

176

to call the shots," she says. So her conscience went back to sleep, smothered under an avalanche of work.

Presently, she was brought up short by an event for which there was no earthly remedy. Her only brother died suddenly and unexpectedly. Gasping with sorrow, she lay on her bed, shattered by a blow so close to her own life. "I sought in the prayer book for some shred of comfort," she says. "I took the Holy Bible from my bookcase where it had lain unread for so many years. But I could find no comfort in either."

Prayer was fruitless, too. "I felt as if each prayer bounced back at me from a high stone wall. I didn't know that the only prayer God will hear from his disobedient and rebellious child is, "God, be merciful to me a sinner, and save me, for Christ's sake."

As her grief subsided, numbed by the passage of time and the finality of death, she began to run again. After a while, she was racing faster than ever through her career as civil servant and housewife. "My job, my home, and my flowers became an obsession," she recalls. "Even my husband received scant attention. Sundays? Sunday became the day on which I worked the hardest."

Religion? She had tried it, and found it wanting. When she inadvertently tuned in a radio preacher, she would spin the dial furiously, throttling his voice. Her head began to ache with pain that pills failed to banish. Nor would long office hours and hard work bring the sleep she needed. Now, her nights were filled with desperate questions.

"Is there really a God, a heaven, a hell? Perhaps everything ends at the grave. Does sin really exist in our modern age?" Not for years had she heard the word in either a sermon or conversation. "Sin, why sin was merely the name of a perfume. The Bible talked of sin, yes, but could one be sure that the Bible was the word of God?"

So the cannonade persisted, its clangor straining her nerves to their limit. One night, she worked late and hurried to the home of a friend to spend the night. She remembers every detail.

"We usually visited in the kitchen, but this night I stopped to rest a bit in the living room. Sinking into a chair, I heard heavenly music. It was a choir, singing. Then an unforgettable voice came on, that of Beverly Shea.

"I loved music and I intended to sit there only long enough to hear the hymns. Before I knew it, Billy Graham was preaching. I had never heard him, but his method interested me. He spoke directly from the Bible and from his heart. Since he was not reading from a script, I tarried a moment longer."

Still, a sermon was the last thing she wanted to hear, so she started to rise. The voice said, "What is wrong with the world? Why can't we solve our problems? Why do people act the way they do?"

He answered his own questions: "The Bible tells us that the human race has a disease called sin. We are sinners by birth because we have inherited this sinful tendency from our parents. We are sinners by choice because when we reach the age of accountability, we choose to rebel against God."

She sank back, aware of her own predicament. As the evangelist continued, she felt as if every word were being spoken directly to her. "Would you like to know forgiveness?" he said. "Then be willing to repent and to receive Christ as your Lord and Master. He will transform your life. You can do it right now."

She remembers, "In my thoughts, I was kneeling again before a candlelit altar of my girlhood. My heart seemed to be melting like wax under the warming strains of 'Just as I am, without one plea.' "

Graham cried, "Wherever you are, if you need Jesus, come! Whoever you are, if you need Jesus, come."

"I come," she whispered.

And a light suddenly shone around her. "It must have been as brilliant," she vows, "as the one that Saint Paul saw so long ago on the Damascus road."

That evening, she embarked on the great adventure that only Christians know. "I committed my life to him without reservation," she says. "I relinquished my will completely, asking, 'Lord, what will you have me do?' "

The answer raced through her mind like prairie fire, commanding, "Love the Lord thy God with all thy heart and soul, with all thy mind, and thy neighbor as thyself. Go back to church, read the Holy Scriptures, pray often, and be a witness to Me."

She recalls that cleansing tears fell most of the night and then: "In the wee hours of the morning I finally slept, and when I awakened I felt as though I had been washed clean by a gentle rain and that I was walking on holy ground. I had the feeling that a hand had been laid on my shoulder and had turned me around in a complete about-face."

Would it last, her incredulous family wondered?

The months passed and the new course of her interests gave answer. Now she spent her spare time serving the Lord however she could, adorning his altar with the flowers that had once been her great vanity, and in tithing and study. "Things that I formerly hated, now I love," she says. "And things that were once my gods are just not important any longer."

When permission to reveal her story was asked, she assented, saying, "I have wanted to shout it from the housetops."

"It is certainly not a pretty story," she adds, "but it is made beautiful to me by its miraculous ending in a conversion so glorious and so final that I belong to Christ for all time and eternity, with no reservations.

"I have wasted many years, for which I am sorry. I hope that God will give me a chance still to do wondrous things for Him. Perhaps the fervor of my testimony can compensate in a measure for the lateness of the hour when I first committed my all to Him."

The end of the great quest is in sight at last for Mabel Duvall, and of her ultimate destination she has no doubt whatever.

God's business begins at sun-up

HE KNEW MOVIE STARS AND BIG SHOTS, HE HAD A PERFECT CHURCH RECORD, BUT WHAT KIND OF SUCCESS WOULD RELEASE HIM FROM THE NAG-GING FEAR OF DEATH?

Ray Davenport had never told any man, but he was desperately afraid of death. Let a real estate prospect bring it up at lunch and he lost his appetite. Let a jokester make a gag about somebody dying and he walked out of the room.

Now he was packing for another business trip. Outside, the warm sun painted the landscape around Whittier, California, a rusty gold. His valise lay on the bed, shirts and socks at one side in a jumble of ties and handkerchiefs. "Where's that Bible?" he thought, stowing his garments. "What did I do with it?" His glance circled the room and he swept it up. "Why do I always take it?" he wondered. Funny how you get into a habit. He had carried it for 27 years now, a holy rabbit's foot. His mind raced back to the farm in Texas where his mother had persuaded him to read the Scriptures from cover to cover. He was then twelve years old. Now he was thirty-nine, riding the crest of a postwar real estate boom. California was growing, his real estate business was booming, and he needed all the luck he could get.

He dropped the Bible into his valise between the drawers and the undershirts and snapped the bag shut. Again his thoughts went back to the farm and his mother and father conducting daily devotions and attending church each Sunday. "Wonder what they would think," he asked himself, "if they knew I hadn't cracked that book for 27 years?"

Prosperity had been a long time coming. Short on education, he nevertheless was fired by a will to win. Early training might have planted the seed. As a boy, he had risen each morning at four a.m. to milk twenty cows. Then he rode a bus twenty-eight miles to Littlefield High School. He went out for basketball and won three letters. He studied hard and became class salutatorian. He did it all the hard way: no radio, no TV, not even electricity, he studied by an old coal-oil lamp.

Until he was twenty, he was a farmer, working cattle and picking cotton. That was the year he decided he wanted to see a big city. He had watched big locomotives pulling shiny cars westward on the Atchison, Topeka and Santa Fe. One day he resolved to become a Californian.

Ray was 25 when he married Dorothy Burnett. With $1,000 in his hip pocket, he and his bride drove out to Palm Springs at the desert's edge, south of Los Angeles. A high mountain's shadow cooled it off every night; after the hot Texas Panhandle it seemed like paradise. They gawked at the palm trees for a day and then decided to settle. Already, a few movie stars had moved into the village and were building homes. Charles Farrell, a former star, had opened a country club with tennis courts and swimming pools. The big-rich had not yet arrived but the celebrity-rich were already there and hunting for fun.

Ray found a bicycle rental business for sale.

"You think we can make a livin' jus' from people renting bikes?" Dorothy asked in her soft, Texas voice. "You wait and see," he promised. "We've got 30 bikes and I bet we'll need more in a year."

He was right. They opened their shop one day and Shirley Temple popped in, asking for a bike her size. Alice Faye and Franchot Tone followed, and Susan Hayward. The big-rich heard about the wonderful Palm Springs air; they came to visit and remained to ride bikes. The Giannini family, owners of the biggest bank in the world, all rode the bikes of "Tex" Davenport, as he was now known. After five years, he owned 119 bicycles and seven motor scooters and had a yearly income of $10,000.

After the war, California land really began to boom, absorbing midwesterners and easterners at a rate that sent the price of building lots skyward. "I think maybe we ought to try real estate," he told Dorothy. "I could go to school at the university and learn appraising."

"If you're going, I'm going, too," she said.

"We'd probably be strapped for a while, but I think this is the coming part of the world."

During the war he had already worked in Whittier, a comfortable town between sprawling Los Angeles and the mountains. It looked like a good spot for people willing to work, so they moved.

"We put in the hours," he says. "I bought a lot on Whittier Boulevard and got aboard the real estate band-

185

wagon. Both Dorothy and I studied nights at the University of Southern California and took out licenses. I worked a 90-hour, seven-day work week. I never saw the inside of a church."

Texas boys are quick to catch on, and Tex Davenport watched every business trick that anybody played in his town. One thing he noticed, and he was not the first, was that all the biggest people had church affiliations. "In Whittier, they belonged either to a lodge or a church," he says, "so our family joined one of our larger churches."

Like countless other young men on their way up, he played the game of churchmanship. "For five years, I never missed Sunday service," he says. "Sure, I considered myself religious."

Sinclair Lewis once wrote of another hard-working real estate salesman named Babbitt. "The content of his theology," Lewis reported, "was that there was a supreme being who had tried to make us perfect but presumably had failed; and that if one was a Good Man he would go to a place called Heaven (Babbitt unconsciously pictured it rather like an excellent hotel with a private garden) but if one was a Bad Man, that is, if he murdered or committed burglary or used cocaine or had mistresses or sold nonexistent real estate, he would be punished. The kernel of his practical religion was that it was respectable, and beneficial to one's business to be seen going to services; that the church kept the Worst Elements from being worse; and that the pastor's sermons, however dull they might seem at the time of taking, had a voodooistic power which 'did a fellow good'."

Tex was invited to attend several meetings of the

186

Whittier Christian Businessman's Committee. Time after time, he saw other Whittier executives and owners of businesses get up and testify to their faith in Jesus Christ and their joyful work in his behalf. He came away shaking his head.

Then he got a notice that a meeting called the Mid-Century Crusade would be held at the Rose Bowl in nearby Pasadena. The speaker would be Billy Graham, a young evangelist who had started brilliantly only two years earlier in Los Angeles, and then gone on to greater triumphs of revival in New England and the South.

"I'd like to hear him," Tex told his wife.

"It's quite a way. The traffic will be bad."

She was right. The traffic was terrible. His seat was high on the side of the monster stadium, but he climbed the slope hoping to hear some message that would allay his doubts.

"I was one of the leaders in the real estate business, and took part in civic activities all over town, but I was empty. I knew I was failing others and others were failing me. It was odd. I'd never smoked or tasted a drop of beer or liquor. I often compared myself with other church members, and felt that I was just as good as they were."

After the preliminaries, Graham rose to speak, and Tex Davenport got a shock. He realized that in all the years of his life, nobody had ever before asked him to accept Christ as his own personal Savior; yet, on the spotlighted platform, a total stranger was talking to his heart as never before. He was stirred deeply, wondering if it was too late now to change his life.

Fifty thousand persons sat about that vast colosseum, straining to hear. "Graham quoted the Bible without making jokes," Davenport remembers. "He talked with such conviction that it brought faith to me. And he asked a question: 'If God spared not the angels, but cast them out of heaven, do you think he will spare you if you neglect Christ and God's Word?' "

He was sitting almost at the top of the Rose Bowl. Hundreds of feet of aisle lay between him and the pulpit. Graham gave the invitation. Tex says, "I was reluctant to surrender." It was too far. It wasn't necessary. He was a church member, a *regular* church member.

He felt a light touch on his shoulder, and a young voice spoke in his ear, urging him to accept Christ. Startled, he slid to the front edge of his seat. Was it to get away from the young man behind him, or to start forward? To this day, he has no idea. But he moved. And then he noticed a gray-haired man directly in front of him. Earlier when Billy had asked for a showing of hands by those who wanted Christ's help, the man had responded.

"They were almost at the last line of 'Just As I Am,' " Davenport says. "Then I bent down and whispered the same encouragement to that stranger I'd got from the chap behind me. We rose up together and started the long walk forward."

On that September night, Tex Davenport remembers, "I felt the conviction and need to surrender my will, my life, my sin and unbelief to Jesus Christ, and to look to him instead of to myself."

A few days later, Davenport astounded his fellow business associates with this simple declaration: "From now on, my real estate office will be closed on Sundays."

"Sunday's the best business day of the week," they remonstrated. "You'll go under for sure."

"Go to church on Sunday, and don't make any appointments for the Lord's day," he told his salesmen.

Before long, his business prospered so greatly that he had to open a branch office.

An even greater change took place in his spiritual awareness. "God became my Father in a *real* heaven," he says. "Now, I could pray in a personal way, trusting Him and feeling He was hearing."

His growth was not all as easy as pie. Bad luck and broken promises often vexed his path, but always God's Word provided a refuge. If trouble showed its head, he merely opened his Old Testament and let the Psalms peal out.

One day, an acquaintance said, "What's your secret, Tex? You sure got something most of us lack."

He answered, "It's no secret. Just read the Book. And then give yourself wholly over to the Lord and let Him make the deals."

"I sure wish I could," the friend said. "Think you might have time to give me some help?"

Soon after that, Ray took the chairmanship of a course of evening Bible classes. Then he quietly embarked on a program of leadership for evangelism in his community. The religious need he had once felt also distressed other people. Moving to a church which supported his beliefs, he and his wife and two daughters enlisted in every good cause they could find. For a year, he went on the air regularly with a program of personal evangelism. From 1956 to 1960, he picked up 600 down-and-outers in Los Angeles' notorious Pershing Square, took them to

189

lunch, and led 149 of them to the Lord. Feeling the need of training others, he wrote a book for classes in man-to-man evangelism that has reached its sixth edition.

Nowadays, when he packs a suitcase for trips, he still drops a Bible atop his linen. But what a Bible it is! Its pages are interlined and marked with many colors, and annotated by strange signs. Its edges are frayed and its type is dimmed from much use.

"In the first five years after I was saved, I read my Bible through seven times and the New Testament through seventeen times," he says. "And I found something new in every single reading."

Business associates demand, "How on earth do you find the time for it?"

He reminds them that once he rose at four a.m. to milk cows. "Now I rise to go about my Father's business," he says.

"And there's one little rule I use that helps considerably," he adds. "Just memorize it, apply it and you'll have no trouble. It's simply, 'No Bible, no breakfast.' "

The fear of death that haunted most of his adult years, what of it? "The wages of sin is death, but the gift of God is eternal life through Jesus Christ our Lord," he quotes.

Can a business man really live by the Book? What of the wheeling and dealing that business demands? What of the corner-cutting and the lies hidden in fine type?

"I'm a Bible bigot," says Tex Davenport, echoing the words of John Wesley when he was founding the Methodist church. "I follow it in all things, yes, in *all* things, great and small."

190

The strength I have, I have from Him

"WHAT WITH MY MENTAL BREAK-
DOWN, MY GIRL GETTING POLIO,
AND MY WIFE LEAVING, I'D HAD
SOME MIGHTY HARD LUCK. . . ."
THEN SOMETHING WONDERFUL HAP-
PENED.

The thin, middle-aged man pressed the document into the minister's hands. "It's a pretty poor effort, but it's about some pretty big miracles," he said.

"If it is from the heart, it's what God wants."

The man said, "I've had some mighty hard luck, what with a mental breakdown, my little girl with polio, and my wife leaving. . . ."

"But you've come through it."

"Oh, I've come through it. I had to learn the hard way. Now that the Lord is in my home, it's as different as night from day."

The minister wrote a notation on the document: "The testimony of Edward R." Here it is as it came to the Billy Graham Evangelistic Association.

My troubles started in 1945, when I got married.

Anyone would expect that a minister's son would be taught the right things, and I was. I was taught not to drink, smoke, or swear, and I was sent to Sunday school, church, and prayer meeting every week. This training was the same as pouring water on a duck's back.

I graduated from our midwestern high school, not with honors, but with several letters in athletics. I thought the world was my oyster. But somehow, I had never learned to spell. It was funny then, but later it knocked me for a loop. Not spelling right, I think, is one of the things that helped defeat me in later life.

Four years later, I became a husband and soon after that a father. We had three children, one daughter and two sons. I worked hard during my twenties. I'd been brought up believing that those who worked hard were those who got ahead. I found out this was not always so.

At home, my inner tensions built up. For one thing, my wife always shut me up when I wanted to express my views. She insisted on making all the decisions. My feelings got to piling up, fighting to be released. I was challenged in everything I said and was not even allowed to correct my children. Then pressure was put on me to bring home bigger paychecks. After a while, I began to suspect that, on top of all this, my wife was pulling away from me. Sometimes, we'd go out to a party and she'd take delight in making me jealous. She was very open about it.

Next, my daughter was stricken with polio. I tried to pray as best I knew how, as any preacher's son ought to know how. But I couldn't find help.

These pressures bore down on my mind over several years. Finally, something had to break. It did—in my mind. I entered a hospital as a mental patient. For three months, I lay there talking and listening and trying to settle down. At the conclusion of their treatments, I went back home.

My wife treated me well enough, but my old boss refused to take me back. I'd had twelve years of aircraft flight line work but it made no difference. He'd given my place to somebody else, and I was out cold. So my wife got a job while I went to barber's college. Then I got a job as apprentice barber.

We were coasting along when my second child got a mysterious leg disease that looked about as bad as the polio. This time, I definitely prayed for help, and sure enough, the leg healed. In the meantime, though, I could sense that my wife had begun to run around. She was working nights as a waitress and I didn't want to believe anything bad but finally I had to. My sister came and told me she knew my wife had been seeing another man.

Now I couldn't trust anyone, nobody, because I'd been deceived by so many people that I once had trusted. I was reading the Bible and hunting through it for help. I had to find an expert to guide me.

That winter, I went back to the mental hospital for treatments. This time, my Bible and all religious literature were taken from me. So you see how bad off they thought I was.

Lying there, I tried to decide whether I should leave my unfaithful wife and the children, or follow the line of least resistance and go back home. If I left, I could get a furnished room somewhere near and see the kids once in a while.

Well, she decided the whole thing by telling me she wanted a divorce. When I did return, she got the divorce but I was awarded custody of the home and my two boys.

Now I began to read my Bible in earnest. I read Billy Graham's column in the local paper and I began to listen to his broadcasts. All my strength was gone, and I became conscious that I had to rely on the Lord for enough energy every day to go to work. I went back to church, to the same old Methodist church where my father had preached, but they gave out a watered-down message that didn't say a thing about salvation.

Through hearing Billy's message, I had learned the Gospel story. This was what I wanted, what I'd been seeking so long. This was truth to trust and believe in. He always repeated, "The Bible says . . ."—and I knew that he wouldn't say so unless it was true.

The verse that hit me hardest was, "Deny yourself. Take up your cross and follow me."

With no helpmate and two boys to raise, how I prayed. One prayer I said was for a Christian lady who would care for my sons while I worked. The Lord answered that prayer very quickly. After a time, I began to pray for a Christian wife. And a few months later, another barber introduced me to a lady who had been through an experience similar to mine. She was trusting and waiting for the Lord to give her a Christian husband and children. We got married in February of 1959, and what a wonderful difference. Now the Lord is in my home and we never have strife. The family prays together and goes to a fine little church we've joined.

By the way, I'd come under conviction that I had to start talking about the Lord and witnessing for him because my time is running out. Well, my witnessing made it necessary for me to quit my job and leave two different barber shops where I worked, but, maybe as a reward, the

196

Lord then gave me my own shop. In it, I keep a Bible and a pile of Christian literature on my bookshelves, and I'm free to witness and say whatever I please.

Looking back, I know that my old nature had no good in it. Only as I yield myself up to the Holy Spirit, keeping myself out of the way, can the Lord use me.

I know also that only the Lord could give me back a sound mind, one that's more sound today than ever before. Yes, all the strength I have, I have from Him.

Some time ago, my wife and I heard that Billy Graham was going to preach in a nearby city. I'd read him and listened to him so long, I had to go. When I saw all those people going forward, I couldn't believe it. It gave me an idea.

The following Sunday, we went back to the crusade with our children so I could take a public stand. I wanted to make my first public stand under the person I felt God had used to bring me to a saving knowledge of our Savior. When he gave the invitation, I went forward to stand with all the others. He didn't know I was there and he'll never know who I am, but what has happened because of him over the years and on that wonderful afternoon has changed my life forever.

A Counterfeit Christian

THEY CALLED HIM A COUNTERFEIT
CHRISTIAN, SO HE PUT HIMSELF INTO
A TEST TUBE, TURNED UP THE HEAT,
TOOK THE ACID TEST, AND FOUND
THAT GRAHAM WAS RIGHT.

When Dr. Nelles Silverthorne, of Toronto, Canada, spoke to God that evening of 1955, he was no whining, cringing, down-at-the-heels sinner. He had everything that life could offer, or so it seemed.

Seeing him among those crusade penitents, fellow citizens said, "There's Silverthorne! He's a scientist. Wonder what he's doing here?"

"Maybe he's conducting an experiment. He's that kind of guy."

He was that kind of guy, always testing, always reaching for the truth ever since he had been taken under the wing of Alan Brown, Canada's foremost pediatrician and creator of one of the world's greatest healing institutions, the Hospital for Sick Children. And now Brown's protégé was seasoned and successful in his own right.

Once, a friend said, "Doc, there's more to life than

you seem to understand. How often do you read your Bible?"

He always had an answer. "Curing sick children is all the righteousness I need," he said, believing it.

But that night at the crusade, he felt a stirring of his mind and heart. He listened with astonishment to the powerful doctrine thrust into his mind by the lean figure on the rostrum. Ministers all over town were debating and quarreling about Graham. Crusades at Harringay in London the previous year and also in Glasgow, Scotland had softened some of their views as they realized he was not a Bible-banging mountebank as some claimed. That Graham refused to profit from his ministry by accepting a salary was now common knowledge. That a local committee ran every detail of the crusade was surely to his credit. But all that was nothing compared to his urgent message.

Silverthorne, raised a Christian, had married and fathered three children, and had become an elder in his church. Nevertheless, he felt he could do worldly things and still believe and attend church and observe the forms of religion. On several previous visits to crusade meetings, he had resisted Graham's challenge. Now the evangelist was saying quietly, "I'm going to ask you to get up out of your seats and come forward. Your friends will wait for you."

Silverthorne's intellect struggled with the impulse to respond as he smiled at his companion who was a Christian surgeon. Reason told him that all Graham had said was right and true, but this going-forward business, why was that necessary?

Graham spoke intently, "You may be a member of a church, a Sunday-school teacher, you may be a church officer. I don't know who you are, but you do need Christ."

That was close to the mark. Elder Silverthorne, baptized at the age of 13, raised in a Christian home, remembered protesting to his mother:

"The religion you are teaching is out of date. It doesn't apply to life today."

Now Graham had called him a counterfeit Christian. He had said that the Holy Spirit possessed the power to transform life. "But you must open your heart and let God in," he insisted.

"I suddenly felt humbled, completely humbled," the physician says. "And I asked the Lord to come in and forgive my sins."

Then the service was over, the last amen pronounced, and the doctor and his confrere rose briskly to join the thousands making their way toward parking lots.

Something had happened back there, something new in his life. He had been told he was a sinner, and the sting of it thrust his memory back to college days.

"I indulged in the usual sins," he remembered. "I neglected the commandments. Yes, there was social drinking, smoking, and all of the other sins so well known to medical students and physicians."

But Billy Graham had not pressed his guilt exclusively on those points. Mostly, he had talked of rebellion against God.

Later, Silverthorne tried to explain it to himself. "My main sin was the fact that I never did know anything about the power of God or the complete change that can take place in a person's life. My head and my heart had been hardened against God. I was going on my own self-righteousness."

Horns honked behind him and tires whined beside him, but he was oblivious, for a vision was lighting his way. Gripping the steering wheel, he felt the growing tension of a great commitment and a total surrender that he had never been able to make. Within, he felt a melting of pride which seemed to leave room for a new and unprecedented resolution.

As the car slowed, his throat worked, and words formed silently, signaling his capitulation. Now, speaking directly to Christ as Master, he said, "This night, Lord, I truly receive you as my Lord and Savior."

"In that instant," he says, "I realized I could never get away again from the meaning of the Bible. I knew it was the Holy Spirit that was planting a message in my heart. I was quite in my right mind as I asked Christ to forgive all my sins, and as I told him I trusted him, and had faith that he would change my life because he had shed his blood for my sins."

So, in that speeding car, a man of science gave himself, by faith, to the Lord, and entered upon an amazing experience.

"The wonder of it is that I did not propose to do too much myself," he remembers. "I felt that this was a change that God would have to make." He continued living his busy life, healing and working, and slowly the change began. "When He came in, He changed my life completely," the doctor says. "And I can report that I have been joyous ever since. God changes your whole bent, your

202

desires, your purposes. He gives you peace and joy in Christ."

Neither Billy Graham nor his associates knew about all this until several years later. One day, a letter arrived at the Association's headquarters in Minneapolis. Its writer was a young woman who had first seen the evangelist during the pioneer telecasts from Madison Square Garden in New York. Now, years later, she was a member of a Christian group in a church near Toronto, to which laymen occasionally came to speak.

Their most exciting speaker, she wrote, was Doctor Silverthorne, of Toronto, who talked to them for more than two hours of the wonders of his changed life. The great miracle of the Christian faith, he had explained, "comes at the point when you ask Christ to forgive your sins, in the moment you completely submit yourself, mind, body, soul and will to Him. The power of the Holy Ghost comes in to you, as Christ actually places Himself in your life."

She went on, "At last I know why Christ said, 'I am the Way, the Truth, and the Life.' My faith means living each day with Christ, who was crucified for my sins; it means Christ living in me and with me. And it means the great hope and promise of eternal life with my Lord and Savior. There is no other hope for the world."

The letter writer concluded by saying, "I'll never forget Doctor Silverthorne's testimony as long as I live."

Now, one of the busiest men in Toronto is even busier as he shares his joy with others. Since that night of surrender, he has addressed hundreds of church meetings and become an active member of the Gideons, the Christian Business Mens Committee, the Pocket Testament League, the Evangelical Medical Mission, and similar organizations.

During the years since his conversion, a person in an audience will sometimes seek him out, asking for an explanation of Jesus' remark to Nicodemus that a man must be born again. "It's true," the doctor replies, quoting John 3:3. " 'Verily, I say unto thee, except a man be born again, he cannot see the kingdom of God.' Christ says that three times."

"But, doctor," they demand, "as a man of science, can you be absolutely sure?"

The seasoned physician smiles as he answers, "As a man of science, I am sure. It's the most convincing experiment I have ever done."

"My life should be happy. Why isn't it?"

A DISCONTENTED MOTHER DISCOVERS
A RECIPE: TAKE AN ORDINARY FAMILY,
POUR IN A FULL MEASURE OF SURREN-
DER, STIR WITH A SMALL PRAYER, AND
SERVE WITH LOVE.

The early spring air was like new wine in St. Paul that Sunday morning as Florine Bernier rose to her feet in the choir loft. The church calendar listed her solo as "I Walked Into the Sunrise." The organ sounded and she began to sing, projecting her message joyously across the crowded pews, up among the eaves of the sanctuary, and out through the budding trees of the church grounds.

As the message formed, a feeling of joy gripped her, as if she were emerging from a dark tunnel "Darkness filled our hearts. 'Twas like a starless night," she sang. "We sought in vain to find our way without a guiding light."

She had been raised in a good home by parents dedicated to Christian Science. They had taught her that unceasing prayer was necessary to reach God and to drive the mind from error which was mortal, to the Spirit which was immortal.

Now, her voice soared exultantly, her words saying: "But suddenly our world was changed; the Lord himself passed by, our lives completely rearranged, and sunrise filled the sky."

That Sunday night, she sat down at a table in her suburban home. The two boys were tucked away and Bob was settled among his Bibles, reading. It had been another good day in their lives. "Happy?" she called.

"Mighty happy," Bob said, with a fond look.

She dipped her pen in blue ink and spun words across the lined letter pad. The moment had been too long postponed. Her fingers raced, released by the elation of her new life. "Dear Billy Graham," she wrote, "We planned to write you for over a year. Now my heart is overflowing with gratitude and I cannot keep it inside any longer. I must share that which I still find hard to believe, which is the story of our conversion."

Florine and Bob had met in a Christian Science Sunday school. Later, their childhood romance blossomed into an apparently ideal marriage. One year after the wedding day, a baby boy was born. Two years later, they received a second son. She remembers thinking, "My life should be divinely happy. Why isn't it?"

How does one catalogue the forces that beset a young couple raising two children in a world so full of puzzlement and agony. Their dissatisfaction seems to have started with absence from their old church, as their social and business obligations grew. Then, as months and years passed, several dear friends and relatives died. Florine began to brood on death.

"You ought to get out more," Bob tried to help.

"How do I manage that, with two children to feed and a house to keep clean?"

"Well, I think you need to see more people. You're forgetting how to laugh."

She felt less reason to smile now than ever in her life. "You could be right," she said. "I think Satan's got hold of my thinking. Sometimes, I wonder if the story of Jesus is just a myth."

"That's what I mean. You're taking things too hard."

"But I'm so afraid of death," she insisted. "I want to be sure we all have a heavenly home."

"Then read your Bible."

She shook her head. "I try, I really try, but I can't understand a thing in it."

He said, "Well, maybe you can get some help somewhere. . . ."

They got help unexpectedly. "I shall never forget that first glorious Sunday at the Billy Graham crusade," she wrote. "My husband had no desire to go with me. But I was there, listening hard as you said, 'God so loved the world that He gave His only begotten son, that whosoever believeth in Him should not perish but have everlasting life.' "

That answer clearly came from Scripture, and it was so plainly and clearly meant for her that she was thrilled to the tips of her toes. "Immediately, I wanted Jesus for my own Savior," she decided. Others might hold back, others might quibble, but not she. All at once she felt pleased that Bob had not come with her. The sermon came to an end with the words of the invitation. She saw that the tall evangelist had laid aside his Bible and was waiting.

"I went forward and accepted Christ," she says. "My entire life changed at that moment of acceptance."

But at home, she found an unexpected wall rising between herself and her husband. "Bob, I want to explain what happened. . . ."

He said, "I don't want to hear about it."

"Bob, please listen to me."

"Thanks, no, Florine!" His face was cold with finality.

So she went softly to her room, recalling the Biblical injunction: "When thou prayest, enter into thy closet, and when thou hast shut thy door, pray to thy Father which is in secret; and thy father which seeth in secret shall reward thee openly."

She told God of her deep hope that Bob might discover for himself what she had learned. "I ached for him to learn the grace of our loving Lord," she remembers. "I felt that I had to make him understand that God's grace would pardon and cleanse us."

So the days passed—with no response from her husband—and then the crusade closed and Billy Graham became a memory except in her thankful prayers. "And then God took over and worked matters out in his own wonderful way," she wrote.

They were relaxing after dinner when they first heard the strong footsteps beyond their front door. "Who

210

can that be?" she said. The doorbell rang and Bob answered it.

The big man said, "Your name was sent to me after the Graham crusade. I'm the minister of the church down the street."

Bob was very correct and polite. "Come in, please."

The visitor was warm and friendly, with a fund of knowledge that embraced many subjects. Bob warmed to his personality, and the minister's interest in his hosts was clearly evident. Finally, it was time to go, and the minister said, "May we have a moment of prayer?"

They bowed their heads, suddenly united by an unexpected loyalty that had not existed until that moment. Then "amens" were said, the visitor bowed himself out, and the door was locked for the night.

"That was quite an experience," she mused.

"And what a likable guy," said Bob, surprisingly. "Let's invite him back."

One dinnertime, Bob asked his wife about a correspondence course of Bible study she was taking. "I might like to take it, too," he said.

Soon, he began to read his Bible, and to seek the company of the minister who had visited them. Some men are brain-pickers, obtaining information through talk and argument as much as from books, and Bob was one of the best. Then, he heard that Billy Graham would be appearing on television for three nights.

"He took in every word," Florine wrote. "And finally he came to understand the peace and joy I had found."

Six months after the crusade, both of them were

baptized and became church members. They had a joint goal, to be more like Jesus. "We both felt reborn. A spiritual love between us seemed to grow by leaps and bounds," she wrote. "We have found an exciting and wonderful common interest. Nothing else is as thrilling to us as discussing the Bible passages we read together."

The growth of a Christian couple is ordinarily not very dramatic, and this tale is no exception. It will satisfy no James Bond fan to follow the Berniers for the next few years, but to those who understand the source of their satisfactions, it may supply a profound thrill. Thirsting for more knowledge, Bob began to seek it at its source, which is the Bible in many translations. He recognized the handicap of his lack of scholarship and enrolled two nights each week in a school of theology. Inevitably, his Baptist brethren elected him a deacon of his church. Later, they made Florine a deaconess, too.

When their pastor moved on to another state, the congregation begged Bob for help. "We want you to lead our services," they said.

"I'm not really up to it," he argued.

"You know more of the Bible than the rest of us," they said. "You can start by running our prayer meetings."

Such an experience could lead in many directions. Presently, its challenge spread through their growing family, calling them to greater understanding and increased service.

Bob probed ever more deeply into theology, preparing himself for the call he felt to become a lay preacher.

The two boys, Tommy and David, accepted the example of their parents and, instead of kneeling hastily for a hurried "Now I lay me down to sleep," they began to talk to God as a friend and constant companion.

Florine's own secret wish came true. "All my life, my fondest dream had been to become a church soloist," she wrote, "but I never had been a member of a church that even used a choir. When we moved, our new church had such a wonderful choir, and I never dreamed I could get into it. Then one day, they asked me to join. And oh, what a joy it added to my life."

A dull story with no murders, no crime, no tension, except the constant stress of Christian growth. Without fireworks or drama, each of its characters accepted new responsibilities and then discovered new talents. Now, the Berniers have made their home into one of God's outposts. Evenings are too short for all they want to do.

Make no mistake about it, they have found their own life of truth. Has it given them the assurance they want? Her favorite song provides this response, and she sings it with thrilling sincerity:

> "We would not trade this joy divine,
> This peace that thrills our soul,
> For anything that once we knew,
> Before Christ made us whole."

What can a reformed wire tapper do?

HARLEM KIDS WERE SO MIXED UP
THEY SHOT HOLES IN EACH OTHER'S
BELLIES, UNTIL JIM VAUS INVITED
THEM TO JOIN GOD'S CLUB.

Jim Vaus was a preacher's son who went sour.

But really sour!

"My most serious offense was armed robbery," he says. "I was committed to prison."

He had the idea that the world owed him a living. God gave him a brain for mathematics and electronics, and he was a whiz kid in communications when World War II came along. He became an Air Force captain. But he still could not tell the difference between what was his and what belonged to someone else. "I misused some government priorities and misappropriated some government property," he explains. A military court martial sentenced him to 10 years at hard labor.

When friends obtained a presidential review of his case, he was pardoned and returned to duty. But the virus of "me first" still circulated in his blood. "The big money end of electronics is wire tapping," he says.

Vaus had set up an electronics shop in Hollywood, and several movie stars hired him to check up on their wives. One day, a short, dapper man swaggered into his place followed by seven henchmen. He was Mickey Cohen, gangland overlord, and he wanted Vaus to locate a microphone in his home. Vaus said he was not interested.

"He pulled out a roll of hundred-dollar bills," Vaus recalls, "and started peeling them off, one after another. My interest suddenly changed and I located the microphone and removed it."

Next, Mickey ordered an infrared fence for his place, an invisible ray that nobody could cross without sounding a buzzer. One night, Vaus and Cohen were in the house when the buzzer cut loose. "We raced into the yard," he says. "I saw a trail of fire sputtering across the grass. It was a lighted fuse. I gave it a yank and a six-inch TNT bomb rolled from under the house."

Cohen figured that Jim had saved his life and showered him with gifts and money. From then on, Los Angeles came to know Vaus as one of Mickey's boys, and after a while as king of the wire tappers. Inevitably, there were complications. Years earlier, he had made some secret recordings for the police, among them a tape of a celebrated madam talking, it was alleged, to the local chief of police. Then he lost it. The newspapers wanted that tape. So did the police. To emphasize their request, Jim was invited to headquarters.

A big man took him into a bare room, where he took off his gun and removed his finger rings. Then he slapped Jim hard.

"Tell me where you hid those tapes," he demanded.

"I've lost them," Jim replied. "I haven't seen them for months." It was the truth. Finally, they let him go.

216

The phone rang at home one day and it was St. Louis Andy. Andy was a gyp who gypped other gyps. "You make me a machine that can pick up race results and hold it for a minute, see, and we'll make a mint, see. . . ." Jim built a wire-tap teletypewriter. "By tapping wires that carried race results," he says, "I could insure a 90-second delay between the moment I got the result and the time that same information would reach the horse parlors."

They worked the racket in Nevada and Arizona. He would rent a room across from a big horse parlor, secretly hook his equipment into the electric circuit, and wait for the big race. When the result came in, he would signal the winner's name to a confederate on the street who would hurry into the parlor and place a last minute bet.

"Then my machine, having delayed the transmission for 90 seconds, would pass on the story of the race and its result. We won every bet."

They got ready to move on to St. Louis and the big money. Andy sent him plane tickets. The electronic equipment was carefully crated.

That night, he and his wife Alice went for a drive and happened to pass the big tent where evangelist Billy Graham was preaching. His name was in all the papers, so they stopped and parked. The only seats left were in the back. They sat through his sermon, drinking it in.

"In college," Jim says, "I determined I would prove that the Bible was wrong. I spent two years trying to do this, yet I came to the conclusion that the Bible was true, that there was a God, that Jesus Christ was the Son of God and the Savior of men. But even though I accepted those basic truths, it brought no change in my life."

In his later work, Vaus always stresses this point:

acceptance of the Bible as truth is not enough. "It is only the acceptance of the person of Jesus Christ," he says, "that brings a total change to one's life."

When Billy Graham asked his audience to give themselves to Christ, Vaus' back stiffened. Alice, sitting beside him, felt his legs brace against the floor and wondered what it portended. Graham said, "There's a man here tonight who has heard this story many times. He is hardening his heart, stiffening his neck, and he's going out of this place without Christ."

"That's me," Vaus thought. Suddenly, all the elaborate defenses he had built caved in and he stood up, stripped of pride, confusedly aware that he could never lick his wickedness without help. He and Alice went forward, along with others, and soon they were in the little prayer tent.

"Kneeling in the sawdust and dirt," he says, "I told the Lord if He thought I meant business with Him, I would appreciate it if he would mean business with me and help me over the hurdles that would lie in the road. It seemed impossible to sever my connections with the crime syndicate, to change my way of living, and to make restitution to those I had harmed."

"What if I have to go to jail?" he asked Alice later.

"If God allows it," she said, "then that would be all right."

Turning around is never easy, but with Jim Vaus it was spectacularly difficult. St. Louis Andy awaited him in Missouri. On the phone, he heard Jim out and said, "Get yourself on that plane, son. Nobody quits me, see."

Big Jim said, "Andy, I can't do it."

He went to the district attorney in Los Angeles and

admitted that he had lied to a grand jury about a police officer, providing misinformation that had brought the innocent cop a prison term. That was perjury. The DA suspected an angle, and sneered, "Now, Vaus, that you've got religion—"

Jim said, "Sir, I didn't say anything about having got religion."

"Well, since you've seen the light."

"Sir, I said nothing about seeing any light."

"Then what did you say?"

"I said that I had accepted Jesus Christ as my personal Savior."

A sympathetic judge put him on probation.

Next, Jim went to an electronic supply house from which he had shoplifted thousands of dollars worth of equipment, gave them a list of the items, and asked for time in which to pay up.

"One day a limousine pulled up in front of my home," he recalls. "Andy and three hoods got out. I said a silent prayer."

Andy snarled, "Let's get goin', Jim. I'm not waitin' any longer."

Jim says, "I told him about the change in me, about the Holy Spirit taking over, and all I was doing to clean up my life. Gradually, his look of contempt changed to one of concern for himself. Suddenly, he called to his friends and they jumped in the car and drove away. I never saw them again."

Los Angeles residents of 1949 will remember some of the headlines that featured Vaus and his regeneration. Even his effort to convert Mickey Cohen made the front pages. He persuaded Billy Graham to visit Mickey's home where the evangelist and the hoodlum drank cokes and talked religion. The attempt was in vain. The gangster's heart was too hard.

Vaus' conversion left him without means of support. What can a reformed wire tapper do? He turned to God, asking for help. He says, "God graciously answered and undertook many things on my behalf."

Organizations began to invite him to speak to other young men in trouble, inmates of prisons and reform schools. Then calls came from army camps, high schools, and colleges. He built a reputation as a lecturer, and enough money came in to keep his wife and four children while he traveled. In the next eight years, he traveled more than a million air miles.

"I was lecturing in a Pennsylvania prison," he says. "I met a teenager who was there for life for killing a policeman. The boy said, 'Mr. Vaus, why do people like you come and talk to us in a place like this? Why don't you reach us before we arrive?' "

Jim had been reading a "Life" magazine story on juvenile crime in New York. His mind lit up as if his skull had been pierced by a laser beam. He hurried to Manhattan and talked to the police, afire with a new idea.

"What's the worst part of this town?" he asked.

They showed him fourteen areas with high crime rates. One was in Harlem, a little over a mile square, holding 190,000 inhabitants. It lay along the strip of East River called Hell Gate. It was the Police Department's notorious 23rd precinct.

Jim walked the streets, sickened by the stench, kicking dead rats into the gutter, stepping over drunks, dodging kids whose bodies had not been washed for weeks, seeing crap games running in broad daylight. Here was where crime began. Here was where human beings became less than human. He made a hard decision. It meant missing years of happiness with his own children and his wife. It meant a life more dangerous than in darkest Africa, with no certainty of success, without pay, without allies or friends.

He would open a boy's club. Maybe—maybe somehow, he could turn a few of those young lives around!

He tells the story, living again through the terror and deprivation of it.

"I found a store in the heart of the slums, rat-infested, vermin-infested, with a floor that was crumbling and a ceiling that was gutted. We fixed it up and moved in furniture.

"I'll never forget that first night. I was scared. Going for a walk, I passed the Hell Gate post office. I saw where people lived, their poverty, their immorality, and I began to realize that these people were living at the very gate of hell.

"I tried to make contacts. Rumors spread that I was working with the New York State Crime Commission. Another said I was the new leader of the Communist party. Maybe my place did look a little strange. We had blacked out the windows with paint, and built a solid wall six inches thick just inside the windows—later I was mighty glad to have it. We took off our glass door and put in solid oak. Then I installed a two-way communications system so I could talk outside, and we even put in closed circuit TV so I could see what was going on out front without having to open up."

He announced that his club was open for business,

and not a soul came. He begged the names of young gang leaders from the police, went to their addresses, climbing up dark stairways. They would tell him, "Oh, he's down on the second floor." In the second floor, they would say, "Sure, we know him. He's up on the top floor." It was a runaround.

Seeking an entree to the kids, he visited a school. It turned out to be one of the city's trouble schools with 2,000 troublemakers. He cornered the dean of discipline and asked for help.

"Who do you represent?" the man demanded.

Jim said, "Nobody."

"Well, who do you work for?"

"Nobody."

"Then, maybe your name's on some approved list?"

"No, not that I know of."

The dean said, "Then, I don't see how we can do . . ."

Jim thrust his big jaw forward. "Wait a minute, sir. I'm not looking for a place to live or a job. I've got a lovely home in California, and a wife and four children. Let me tell you why I've come to Harlem. . . ."

His story was as old as Christianity. He explained how, in a tent in Los Angeles, he had found Christ. And now he wanted to help others do the same thing. The dean heard him out and said, "Well, maybe you might come and see me again tomorrow."

No teacher in that school had ever met anybody like big Jim, a guy who wanted only a chance to serve the defeated young people of the 23rd precinct. They inspected him like a man from Mars: first the school psychiatrist, then the school psychologist, and finally the principal.

"They granted me the privilege of conducting a school assembly," Jim says, gratefully. He unpacked some of the electronic gear he had brought east, stuff that would make a man's hair stand on end, all tried out and perfected in hundreds of lectures. His show lasted forty-five minutes. The kids bought it. And they bought Jim Vaus. He said, "Come on down to my club and I'll teach you all kinds of tricks."

They came, bringing their troubles, as he had hoped they would. He built a pint-sized counseling room, where he could sit with a boy or girl and listen to their agonies, and do his best to help. He lived alone in a tiny, single room behind the club kitchen, with a quarter-bath. Much of the time, he had no idea where his next meal was coming from. Slowly, friends began to contribute funds, but money was not the most important thing in those beginning days. Delinquency is not caused by lack of money.

"There are two factors," Jim says. "First, lack of love. Second, lack of discipline. We try to add both love and discipline to their lives. We try to win their friendship. We do this by appearing with them in court when they're in trouble. We help with their problems at home, providing dental and medical care. We try to win their confidence, and eventually we win a hearing for the Gospel. Strangely enough, we have almost never conducted a worship service within the club."

Slowly, the hostile climate changed to respect and dependence. The single clubroom became too small. Jim was forced to become a corporation named Youth Development, Incorporated—or YDI, as all the cops in Harlem know it today. Now, three clubs are open, one for girl gangsters. His staff consists of eighteen paid workers plus forty volunteers. When Billy Graham visited New York some time ago, Vaus got 123 juvenile gang leaders together to hear him.

"I've never seen a group sit so still, listen so quietly, and be so visibly moved," he says. "It's something to see those rough, hard kids who've handled knives and guns and chains, sit there with tears literally running down their cheeks. And when Mr. Graham gave the invitation, better than half of them responded in giving their hearts and lives to Jesus Christ. We've followed them up with a Sunday-school class I teach on Sunday mornings and two classes during the week."

Has it helped? Have lives been changed? Have those changed lives changed the hard-nosed, crime-ridden 23rd precinct?

The New York Children's Court reports that juvenile crimes have dropped by forty percent in the area. *Time* magazine found that gang killings had dropped from twenty-three per year to ten, the first decrease in many years.

Lieutenant Louis Cottell, Detective in Charge, 23rd precinct, says, "YDI came to Harlem in the person of Jim Vaus. It came unknown, unheralded, and poor. It came not to badger, not to preach with empty mouthings, but to preach by example the love of God and His Word. It came to say to kids who were so mixed up they were shooting holes in the bellies of their playmates, 'Let us help you. And as long as you try, we'll stand in back of you.

224

There's only one way. God's way. We know because we've tried them all.'

"What else does this mean?" Lieutenant Cottell went on. "It means we have gone eighteen months at a stretch without a juvenile gang shooting. It means we haven't had a kid 'shivved' in the back, lying dead in the gutter. It means I haven't had to climb so many creaky tenement steps to tell mothers that their sons are dead. Instead of dealing with wild kids, bent on self-destruction, the Police Department is beginning to see young ladies and gentlemen emerging."

Of the fifty odd gangs in the precinct, Vaus now works with more than half. Eleven of the first twelve boys who became club members six years ago have developed into fine, young citizens. All have jobs, one or two are married, one works in a bank where he supervises nineteen other employees. But for the grace of God and Jim Vaus, all of them, almost certainly, would be in prison or on public relief roles.

Today, Big Jim is one of the most respected figures in the 23rd precinct. When he walks down the street he usually trails a covey of juveniles behind like a modern Pied Piper. His three clubs and his summer camp and his training school can reach only about 150 boys at one time in the depth that is needed for their regeneration. His waiting list is long and urgent, and his dreams keep bubbling.

Next, he hopes to establish a Boys Town here in the East. The need is pressing. Without love and without discipline, the slum-bred youth turns almost automatically to crime. And the wages of sin, Jim knows, is death.

Recalling his days as a Mickey Cohen henchman,

he ticks off his old California associates: "Sam Rummel, Mickey's mouthpiece, murdered. Neddie Norbert, murdered. Hookie Rothman, murdered. Little Dave, vanished. Farkas, vanished. Hap Meltzer, in prison. Mickey Cohen, in prison."

People say, "Big Jim, you sinned. How come you got off so easy?"

He has two answers:

"When Christ died on the Cross," he says, "He paid with His life for all my sins. When I turned my life over to Him, God forgave me. That settled it.

"Second, there's a Proverb that may account for what's happening to my clubs. You look it up," he challenged visitors.

It reads: "When a man's ways please the Lord, he maketh even his enemies to be at peace with him."

226

Drawn into the circle

BOB PEERMAN DETESTED GOODY-GOODIES, YET THERE HE WAS AGAINST HIS WILL, SINGING HYMNS AND TALKING RELIGION.

His brother can be blamed for the whole thing. He was the one who brought back that brochure from the conference of Christian laymen. He thrust it at Robert E. Peerman, president of Peerman Homes, of Corpus Christi, Texas.

"Read it," he said. "You might learn something."

Bob saw a photograph of men standing around in a circle. They were holding hands and he felt a giggle rising in him. They all looked like "goodies," and he had a vast contempt for "goodies."

"Well, that's just darling," he said. "But let's get on with our business."

Bob's knowledge of Christianity you could stick in your eye. "They're suckers. Weak individuals trying to show others how good they are," he thought.

Bob had a religion and a god—himself!

229

"Everything was 'me first,' " he says. "When I met someone, I would think 'What's this guy gonna do for me?' "

If he figured he could come out with some benefit, he became friendly. If not, he turned his back. He had only a few friends and wanted no more. "I really didn't like people that much," he says.

His temple was called the First National Bank. People knew this about him for he never bothered to hide it. "He rates everybody by the amount of money they have," they said. "He's out for all he can get."

"It was a form of pride, I guess," Bob says. "I had fine children and a beautiful wife and we had a swinging crowd. We were the best twisters in town. I had my own airplane. We did about anything we wanted to do."

So twelve months passed, and Bob's beautiful wife said, "Let's go to that Bible conference this year." She had seen the folder with its picture of the people holding hands, and something down deep responded to their singularly fresh and joyous faces.

He says, "I fought her with everything I had. I said, 'Well, sure I'll take you . . . !' " but he planned to be certain that something would come up. When it did, when he explained it carefully, she stopped him like a line-backer. "We're going," she said. They did.

He struggled all the way. Driving to the conference city, he tried hard to get lost. He ran over things hoping to get a flat. They came to a lake and he purposely made a wrong turn to the right. She said, "Honey, you're supposed to turn left."

But he tricked her and after a while she said, "Honey, it's getting dark and we are lost."

230

They finally arrived late and the first person they saw was one of Billy Graham's close friends and co-workers, Howard Butt, a grocery chain executive who has been an evangelistic assistant in several crusades. Peerman says, "I didn't like him because he was king of the goodies."

Their first meeting was worse than Bob had anticipated. All religious talk, and nothing about business and the world going to hell. The leader sat everybody in a circle and said, "Each person introduce himself and say why he came."

Bob laid it on the line, brash and bitter. "I'm here because I was 'drug'—he gestured toward his beautiful wife—"and I don't believe any of this religious bit. It doesn't make any sense. To me, it's got to be reasonable. Two and two have got to make four or I can't buy it. I think you're a bunch of people standing around trying to be good."

There it was, both barrels; and some of the eyebrows in that circle rose right up to their bald spots. Nobody answered back and Peerman got to feeling good about the kick in the teeth he had given the goodies. Then a compact, powerful-looking fellow got up and began to talk on self management. That was Dr. Fred Smith,* one of the leading scientists in America.

Bob recalls, "They ran him out on the floor and he gave a brilliant talk on how to operate a business, comparing it with Christianity." Businessman Peerman ate it up, grabbing at all the two-plus-twos that Smith laid before him. Then he hurried his wife back to the hotel and began to scribble notes like mad. She said, "Well, what's this all about?"

* The story of Dr. Fred Smith is told on page 163.

"This guy has just given me the greatest idea on how to run my business I've ever come across," Bob beamed. She was a smart wife. She said nothing.

So the conference went into its second day, and that night the speaker was a merchant named Gabe Payne, who told how the king of the goodies, Howard Butt, had led Payne to Christ and changed his life.

"I told my wife," Bob says, "oh, I've got to hear this cat. Boy, I've got to see the thunder and lightning he's supposed to have."

Butt talked on the third night. Peerman sat out front, waiting. "I sit back in the chair with my arms crossed and I put this big smile on my face and I just think, 'Okay, I'm waiting for you, man. Show me some of that thunder and lightning.' "

The talk lasted thirty minutes. "And sure enough, there was thunder and lightning all over the room," Bob says.

It wasn't a sermon, it wasn't an address, but it was the sort of talk that made Bob think. Butt said that Jesus Christ was the Son of God, and this was a little hard for him to take. He remembered that Fred Smith had recommended that if you get something real tough to understand, just hold it in your mind and work it over. Bob did that.

"I worked it over and I thought, well, there might be a God, and He must be powerful. Howard had told how Christ said he would come and live with me, and I wondered if maybe I could be related somehow to this power. That thought really shook me. I left there with my own religion wrecked."

For the first time in his life, he faced up to what he

might do if things in his personal and business life really got tough. "I was afraid I wouldn't be able to take it," he says. "So I went out and talked to some of those people. They didn't talk to me about money. They just talked about God."

Next, he sat in with one of the groups that was studying problems that Christians face in business. Before the meetings were over, he had found a new religion. "I did accept Christ as my Savior," he says. "It was an experiment in faith, because if all I'd heard was true, it was sure worth a good try."

Since that night, over two years have passed. "Everything is just exactly as Jesus Christ said it was," he says. "He has really changed my life because He changed my way of thinking. In everything I do now as a Christian, well, I'm kind of out of it. Someone else is running the show."

Bob Peerman changed in other ways. "People now have become more important to me. I finally realized they are sons of God and God loves them; they are people, not just things, or painters or electricians.

"It's given me an honesty I never had before. I was honest in the world's view, I guess. I didn't steal. I wouldn't cheat. My trouble was that everything was 'me first!'

"You know, I'd had a lot of trouble with my stomach, and I don't have that kind of trouble any more. I'm not worrying all the time.

"Our family life? Boy, there's a different relationship between my wife and me. I was sort of her god, and, man, that's tough. To be relieved of that was a real blessing."

Other changes happened gradually. The children came to take more of his time and attention. "They don't belong to us," he says. "They belong to God. God gave them to us to love and to guide a while. Understanding this has made a lot of difference."

"Now you won't believe this," he adds, "but it has even changed my golf. Yessir, it has taken six strokes off my game."

So the skeptical businessman who thought all Christians were goodies, found himself drawn into the circle of fellowship of those who have grown through the influence of Billy Graham and his evangelistic enterprises. And the circle of the righteous was enlarged by the addition of another soul.

"I've still got problems," Peerman says, "but it's wonderful how faithful Christ is. I stumble off on my own for a while and I come back and He says, 'Well, I'm glad to have you back, you silly thing.' Or I'll start the day and say, 'Lord, I give you this day,' but by 8:30, I've taken it back, and he says, 'Go ahead, man, and see if you can do it!' About 8:45, I'm stumbling around again and, if I'm smart, I just say, 'Okay, Lord; it's all yours.' And then it sails."

The false gods are gone, the counterfeit worship, and the phony evaluation of others. Peerman is so grateful, he keeps wondering what he can do for God, and this finally brought him to the greatest discovery of all.

"I can't do anything for Him, really," he says, "except to love Him, and that is what He keeps telling me, because that's all He wants me to do."

234

Part Three

Their
letters

They bring problems and gratitude, confessions and questions—and a joyous sense of new peace and power.

They say that they've been born again!

"As one, we two rose in our living room."

I'm afraid, when it comes to watching television and listening to radio, I am "untouchable." I am very hard to reach, and show no emotion. However, while watching and listening to you recently, I got hit *very* hard. You, and Jesus, hit me like I have never been hit before. When you called for people in the stadium to stand up for Jesus and be counted and written in the book of life, and seeing the fine response, I got all choked up. When they began pouring on the field, as the raindrops were pouring from the heavens, I got goose pimples and had tears in my eyes. Although my wife and I were not with you in body, we were in heart and soul. Just as one, we two rose in our living room. You have saved two more souls for Christ.

R.G.
MADISON, WISCONSIN

"My people are pagans."

Sir, as a newborn Christian during your Africa tour, I have repented of my sins and asked God's forgiveness. I am sure He has already done so according to my faith in His Word. Sir, my people are *pagans,* but I am eager to develop my own life and my family as well in Christ.

O.T.U.O.
Lagos, Nigeria

"I made a cross in the field by the irrigation ditch."

I have experienced the most joyous moment of my life this afternoon. I found God!!! I read an article in *Decision* in which the author said you must give ALL your heart to God. I guess this was my key to God.

My brother and I made a cross out in the field by an irrigation ditch. We have gone out and prayed together a few times early in the morning when the sun was coming up, so we could see the wonders of God. (My brother is seventeen and I am sixteen.)

Today I committed my life to God. The moment I did, joy leaped into my heart. I was so happy I could hardly stand it. I know that my name is in the Book of Life!

I want to thank you and your staff for your wonderful paper and for helping me find God.

C.K.
Fort Collins, Colorado

"From atheist to Jesus Christ."

I have just recently been converted from an atheist to Jesus Christ. Please send me any information that you think will give me strength and faith after about forty years of darkness.

L.P.
CALIFORNIA

"We are separated by jail term."

Because of your telecast, I receive Christ in my heart & it give me the strength to find Christ & you teach me to not sin, resist temptation not only of adultery, but of other sins as well. I stand & I took Christ in my heart. I repent, I acknowledge my sins, & I receive Christ.

My husband has broken the law & we are separated by jail term. He said he had found Christ there and he gave himself, his whole life, to Christ. I feel good to give myself also. May God bless your wonderful works.

B.G.
ROCHESTER, PA.

"I sent for a Testament in Hebrew."

I always looked on the people who said they were Christians as very foolish. But thank God, I saw the advertisement in one of the magazines about the meeting to be held in Windsor Park football ground, Belfast.

I went to hear Mr. Graham for myself, and after the talk he gave on God's holy Word from the New Testament, I was very much upset. Then I began to think that for myself the best thing to do was to send for a New Testament in Hebrew, as it would give me the truth about the salvation in Jesus' name.

When I read the narrative of the Cross—that the holy child Jesus was the Jewish Messiah the scales dropped off my spiritually blind eyes. I now know the truth about the Savior of all men, Jew and Gentile. I still love my Jewish people and will keep praying that the Holy Spirit will convince them about the Savior Jesus Christ being their Messiah whom they are still awaiting.

C.I.
LONDON, ENGLAND

"I hold a Ph.D.—I've just been released from a mental hospital."

I have just been released from a mental hospital where the doctors have successfully treated me. I lost my job six months ago. I hold a Ph.D. degree and was a professor of microbiology at a university, investigating the treatment of certain types of cancer. I was held in some esteem by other scientists throughout the nation and in some foreign countries. My neighbors liked me, but I hated myself.

Now I have been able to let my pride go and to

240

come to Jesus as a little child with faith instead of trying to understand intellectually. Tonight I heard your television broadcast of the Chicago crusade and have finally accepted Jesus Christ as my Redeemer and Savior.

P.E.
MILWAUKEE, WISCONSIN

They write about the ones they love.

"We were an average couple, drinking, telling lies."

We were an average married couple who enjoyed the things of the flesh: drinking, telling lies where the truth would not hurt us. We had no spiritual blessings whatsoever and did not attend any church. Religion was a banned subject at my mother's home when my husband and I visited. Our home was just a sleeping place and we had hardly any visitors. Altogether we lived a selfish life. We took our meals at separate times, we never said grace, and there was no prayer life at all in our home.

God took control on June 1, and as I went forward on that windy night of the crusade, it was like being reborn. The following morning things looked quite different, and I tried to get my husband to come on Saturday to listen to the choir, as I had never heard anything so beautiful before. He did come along, with my mother and father, and when Billy Graham said, "Are you for God or against him?" he knew he was on the Lord's side. You can

241

imagine the joy we felt; it was as if we had been married again.

Since then many wonderful things have happened to us. Our home has a resident visitor—God. We gave up drinking, which didn't seem hard to do. I do not know what it is to swear now. Lies have disappeared from our lips, and we love going to my parents' home. Now we have friends who come to see us often. We have given our testimonies together in church and have helped to start a youth group. Donald has also given his testimony at another church. I am a member of Young Wives and my husband attends Bible study classes.

We have had our times of doubt, but with God's help they have been overcome. We thank God for sending Billy Graham and the Team to England.

Mrs. A.L.H.
FARNSWORTH, ENGLAND

"I had filed for divorce."

Believe me, I had filed for divorce—but with my family, and all their teenage neighbor friends, we sat together in front of the television set eating popcorn and drinking cokes, and listening to your every word. After the third telecast last night, we all prayed together. And we are staying together!

THANK YOU—THANK YOU.

THE O. FAMILY
COVINGTON, KENTUCKY

242

"We were at the end of our rope."

Last evening my wife and I heard your last sermon. Your subject was "The Home," on Husband and Wife responsibilities. This sermon came at a time when we were at the end of our rope. Your sermon really brought out how so often I have neglected my responsibilities to my Lord, wife, and children. My job in the USAF has demanded that I be away from home much more than I really wanted to. My wife has never accepted the way of life I elected. She has not been strong enough to carry out her responsibilities, and she feels that I elected the wrong way. As a result, she turned to alcohol and resentment. We both know this is not the way God wants things to be. She is going today to try to get help for her drinking and a new look on life. Will you pray for her and this family and ask God to shine his light on us. I pray each day in my own little way that things will change. I know that I have not served the Lord as he desires, but your sermon last night surely gave me a shot in the arm.

J.A.M.
GEORGIA

"I never expected such results."

I was one of your ushers at Madison Square Garden in 1957, the son of a Baptist minister. While visiting England at the age of seventeen, I was converted during one

243

of your services in Harringay, London. I naturally awaited your visit to New York with enthusiasm.

However, I never expected such results within my own family and in New York City as a whole. My mother and my younger brother, age fourteen, made their decisions soon after the beginning. My smallest sister, Jo, is the nine-year-old girl who went forward before anyone else on the second television night. At the time of her conversion she was sitting alone in the service. My father tried later to tell her that she didn't understand all of it, but she said, *"Neither does Billy Graham!"*

L.Y.

NEW YORK, NEW YORK

"My husband was almost an alcoholic."

My husband and I haven't been Christians long. We were saved last summer when the Chicago crusade was on television.

We didn't start watching it until the third night, when you preached on David and Goliath. That night I gave my heart to Christ and told my husband I intended to go to church and to bring up our two boys right.

Two nights later as my head was bowed in prayer, my husband tapped me on the shoulder and said, "Billy Graham is right. We have been living a sinful life and we are going to change it." I am so glad that we have a God of emergency, because my prayer was answered just then.

We sat up that night until after midnight, discussing the things we had done wrong and how we should

244

change them. Then we went to bed and it was as if Jesus was standing there. The next Sunday we started looking for a church home. We found it, and we are now attending a Nazarene church.

We were married when I was fifteen and he was twenty, and our marriage went on the rocks. My husband was almost an alcoholic. Now Christ has taken away the desire for alcohol and has saved our marriage. We have testified to our neighbors and friends, but many of them just don't understand.

T.L.
CALIFORNIA

"My daughter said, 'I hate you.' "

I have been attempting to reach the heart of my daughter, now approaching fifteen. She has said to me, "I hate people, I hate you, I hate everyone." It has come from her lips, clearly, calmly, coldly, without anger but with all sincerity. I am 46 years old and I have never experienced such a feeling in my own heart.

To know only love for one's child and to behold this hostility in her is to see love lie bleeding. I cannot account for this seed in her, I cannot see the hand that planted it, but I can see the bright Finger that traces my path for me in this. I have failed, not by immoral example, not by callous disregard of "duty," but by forsaking the battle that justice and loving discipline must wage against the intruder. I abhor dissension and anger.

Now, however, my terror has been transformed. I

245

hear the whisper of duty, of love's gentle firmness, and her cries of "unfairness" and "all the others are" I shall now endure with serenity. She will suffer, for I have taken away some of her freedom. She tells me, "It won't work, I'll rebel."

My reply? "I love you; God bestowed a duty on me in loving you. None of your tears, tantrums or temper shall again prevail against me. Rebellion will only deprive you further. I hold your life, ten years hence, in my hand this moment. Neither you nor society shall prevent my love from serving you."

Thank you for your cup of strength.

A.A.A.
WISCONSIN

"Pray for us just once, please."

How do I say thank you? I am 22 years old and a mother of four wonderful children. I've been married almost 8 years and have been a Seventh-day Adventist for four of those years. My husband has lived his own life of wine, women and song all these years and our marriage is just about gone or maybe I should say was almost gone.

Monday night my husband came home just in time to hear the last half of your sermon (the first one). He was so very drunk I was afraid he would make me turn it off. By the time you made your closing call, my husband was in tears. For the first time ever, we knelt and prayed together. The next day I prayed all day for him, but when he came home, sober this time, he watched your program and never said a word. The next night was the same. I was afraid the actions of Monday night were merely the reactions of a man that was drunk and that it had really meant nothing. Therefore, on Thursday, I decided that if my husband could sit through those three wonderful sermons and still remain unmoved except while intoxicated, then no one could reach him and there was no more reason to stay with him. So all day I prepared myself to tell him that I was going to leave.

Before I had a chance to say anything, he came to me and told me he was going to change. He said the Lord was calling him and he could no longer deny His voice. He wouldn't tell me all he planned to do, only that this Sunday he is going to church with his mother again. My only note of sorrow is he is not including me in his plans. Our religions differ but I told him I would back him 100 percent if he gave his life to Jesus Christ. I would attend church with him anywhere he wanted to go and would never try to press him into mine. God has done so much already I know that He will help us through this too.

We are sending a small contribution. Mr. Graham, if I had a million dollars, I would send it just so you could remain on television. Thank you for your dedication and your ministry. Thank God for his love and forgiveness. Pray for us just once, please.

Mrs. S.D.
Texas

They write as fathers, mothers, parents

"All of a sudden, my son is arrested."

Thank you, Billie Graham, for your message. You touched my heart, just when I needed it so desperately, when it seemed like there was no hope in all the world— and took me back to when I was a little girl, when my Father and Mother were members of the Salvation Army.

My son who has been so wonderful thru the years, with a family of his own now, a wonderful job, a perfect army record, a major in the reserve, a college graduate, all of a sudden my son is arrested for larceny with his company. I tell myself it can't be true. He is sentenced to one year in the county jail, and would be much more but for the fact he had such a good record until now.

My Mother, who is a Christian, tells me that many have fallen to temptation and God will undertake to give our boy another chance. So you see, when it seemed like there was no hope, your message helped me and now I have hope. Thank you.

MRS. F.J.
WASHINGTON

"It is wonderful how she testifies."

After watching your program last evening, I had to write and tell you how inspired and deeply moved my husband and I were listening to your messages. We were both raised in Christian homes and we have been Christians all our life and we try to do our best, but after hearing you again we realize that there is still much more to be done in our home. We have a son three years old and our baby son is one month old, and we ask an interest in your prayers that we might be even better parents in the future than we have been in the past. I would also like to mention that when I went to the hospital to have my baby I roomed with a Catholic lady who has been writing to you. She lost an eight-year-old daughter and it is wonderful how she testifies to others about finding God and how much you, Mr. Graham, have helped her.

Mrs. C.L.C.
Leechburg, Pennsylvania

"I was like a new person."

I was a news reporter for a large metropolitan daily, sent to cover the Graham meeting in Boston back in 1950. Something struck me and I could not get away from it for seven years. In the summer of 1957 my son was converted at the New York crusade. I watched the meetings on television, and the combination of seeing Mr. Graham and witnessing the change in the life of my own son, finally drew his mother and myself to hear the evangelist. When I started to walk down the aisle of Madison Square Garden a great change came over my life. I still can't explain it, but I was like a new person.

D.S.
Miami, Florida

"A clear cut stand on morality."

Thank you for taking a clear-cut stand on morality. As a father of five and a Catholic, I have said the same things many times to my children. The privilege and dignity of man's or woman's sexual need for each other can only come thru love and be blessed by marriage. In this day of, "What can we get away with," it's very good to hear someone like you lay down the law, as God intended it to be interpreted. God bless you.

E.P.P.
Jackson, Michigan

They tell of ills unmasked, of sorrows blunted

"We didn't realize that our child was only God's loan."

At a crusade meeting in Richmond several years ago, I was compelled to answer the Lord's call and dedicate my life to him. Not too long after, I married a fine Christian boy. A year later the Lord blessed us with a beautiful baby daughter. We felt that our happiness was complete and secure, but we did not realize that our child was only God's loan to us for a short time. When He took her back to Himself we were filled with bitterness, and I am ashamed to admit that we turned away from God and sought refuge in other things. We both tried to put it out

250

of our minds. We thought that remembering would only bring suffering and pain.

Last night I watched and the message impressed me with the fact that God did not withhold worldly suffering from His only Son. Therefore suffering is a privilege. Last evening, for the first time since her death, I was able to talk of my child, of her beauty and goodness, and feel nothing but peace and the sense of having been greatly blessed.

So thank you for all you have unknowingly given me, for making my mind and heart receptive to the Lord's will.

B.W.S.
NORFOLK, VIRGINIA

"I am an unwed mother-to-be."

Your program on morals has given me more self-assurance than any appointment with my social worker at the Children's Aid Society.

I am an unwed-mother-to-be, eighteen years of age, and sadder but wiser. My childhood consisted of a series of foster homes and unhappiness. However, I am more thankful than regretful for my past. It has given me maturity, compassion, and understanding of others around me. I hope to keep my baby, not out of selfishness, but out of deep love for it. God will surely give me the strength to bring up a fine citizen. Despite my lack of marital status, I *know*, deep in my heart, I have strength enough to do this.

251

church. I kept getting more miserable both physically and mentally. My conscience became almost unbearable. Then I learned I had multiple sclerosis, a paralyzing disease with no cure. This, along with my conscience, seemed more than I could bear. I was in constant fear and anguish. I tried alcohol and everything else, but nothing seemed to help. Then I saw your program on television.

I renewed my faith and gave my life to God. Suddenly my life began to have meaning and purpose again. I still have the disease and am under treatment, but I have not had a serious attack since the day I went to God for help. I am able to face life again and the fear is gone. My work also has new meaning. Maybe I can help others know that they, who are afflicted, can find a new life through Christ.

E.A.
KANSAS

"The more I hurt others, the smarter I thought I was."

For many years I had been a very heavy drinker, so that I was on the verge of becoming an alcoholic, but by the grace of God, I am saved. Apart from this dreadful habit, I had a very filthy tongue and a violent temper. In fact, while under the influence of alcohol I have broken windows and smashed whatever I could put my hands upon, doing great harm not only to my home but to myself, physically and mentally. The more violent in drink, the more I hurt others and the smarter I thought I was—until at last, with nothing worthwhile to live for, I wanted to commit suicide.

254

Then the miracle happened. A Christian lady living nearby begged me to go with her to the Graham crusade. Merely out of curiosity I went. Some compulsion urged me to go forward and give my life to Christ, for nothing else had helped me. I thought at least I will give God a chance. A strange peace came over me. I began reading the Bible, commenced going to church, joined a prayer group, and the Lord Jesus really came into my heart and life and cleansed me from all my sins.

It is now nearly three years since I have touched any strong drink of any kind whatever, and the temptation to use vile or depraved language has disappeared. In great gratitude I write this humble testimony of my conversion. Should anybody reading it or hearing of it feel in the depths of despair, there is nothing in this world to do other than to go down on one's knees and humbly accept the Savior and His salvation and praise Him forevermore.

MRS. I.M.R.
BONDI, AUSTRALIA

"And then the Lord gently took her."

Thought you would like to know that my mother, Mrs. Ella B. Good, almost eighty-four, asked me if I thought she was too old to sign up for the crusade counseling course. She wanted to know all she could to help bring people into the Kingdom.

I urged her to sign up. She attended the first meeting at our church (First Presbyterian, Hollywood), and then the Lord gently took her to be with Him. We found

255

her crusade counselor training book, memory verses, and Bible in her bed by her side.

She seemed to skip the earthly pangs of death, so that she could celebrate the most glorious Mother's Day she had ever known.

(MRS.) R.H.P.
LOS ANGELES, CALIFORNIA

They write of faith renewed and lives rededicated

"I had been living a lie."

Ten years have passed since that wonderful night in 1954. Almost any other night, the seats at Harringay Arena would have been full but a heavy rain threatened. I took my place high in the gallery.

My impression was of vastness and of the sea of faces. I had no premonition that I was shortly to make the most momentous decision of my young life. To put it simply, on that night I met Jesus. He called me, and I responded. The fact overlooks, however, the terrific battle of wills that took place.

You see, I did not want my family to know that I had been living a lie. As the appeal went forth, I knew, if I went forward, everybody would know that Pat Currey, the Sunday-school teacher, youth worker and choir member had been a sham and a phony.

Yes, for the first time I realized that, despite my

256

busy church activities, I was still an old-fashioned sinner. And the point on which my salvation depended was: would I confess Christ openly?

I can remember quite clearly putting my hands under my seat to hold me there so I would not go forward. But I rose—I had to rise—and I yielded all to Christ.

That was ten years ago. It would take too long to tell you about answers to prayer, daily blessings without number, and His constant presence and peace. I can only say, "Thank you Lord. Praise be to God."

P.C.

LONDON, ENGLAND

"I have become so busy . . . that I have missed my God."

I teach Sunday school, I am vice president of our women's society, I am chairman of "character and spiritual education" in our PTA. But I have become so busy putting on programs, talking, and trying to find appropriate materials, that I have missed my God!

I took your invitation to ask Christ into my heart, for I was distraught at seeing what I had become. When I knelt and said, "Take my life," the tears and the anguish left me and I was at peace. It came to my mind that this was the first time I had ever been on my knees without asking for something. I said, "Take me," not "Give me guidance," or "Make me a better mother," or any one of a hundred different prayers I have been using to bolster myself up and make myself look good.

257

You made me see myself as I am, and I thank God from the bottom of my heart.

(Mrs.) F.T., Jr.
Florida

"I realized I had not surrendered my all."

I thought that I knew Christ as my Savior until I heard your message, but I realized I had not surrendered my all to him until now. I got on my knees after hearing you speak, and I want the Lord to have full surrender of my life today. I am a church member and have been for a good many years. But I just had never found the Lord until now.

Mrs. L.M.
Alabama

"I rededicated my life. It was a miracle."

Tonight, during the second telecast of the San Diego crusade, I watched as hundreds of inquirers came forward in the streaming rain at the close of the service. In that group I saw a young sailor and I thought of myself when, as a young sailor back in 1946 or '47, Billy Graham invited me and several others in uniform to testify on the platform during a Youth for Christ rally at the Moody Memorial Church in Chicago.

For many years I enjoyed a victorious life in Christ but then several years ago I fell victim to the so-called "higher criticism" espoused by Renan, Loisy, Bertrand Russell, and others.

Like Peter, I had denied my Lord before men; but even as Peter was warned by the crowing of the cock, I was warned by the 3-part article, "God is My Witness," by Billy Graham, which appeared in *McCall's* magazine.

It is a joy for me to be able to tell you that on the 30th of April with much earnest prayer and the help of the Holy Spirit working through those articles in *McCall's*, I rededicated my life to my Lord and Savior, Jesus Christ. It was a miracle in the fullest sense of the word; Christ now lives in me, and I in Him.

R.R.

KENT, OHIO

"Christ goes with me to the research lab."

This evening my wife and I heard Christ speaking through you, and when you gave the invitation to come and to allow Christ to live within our hearts, we found ourselves rededicating our lives to him.

Although I bore the name Christian for many years prior to marriage, I did little in the way of living a Christlike life. I know God loves me, for he gave me my wife, a Methodist minister's daughter and a dedicated member of the "company of the Committed." My life has been so changed by Christ through her that it would take pages to share all the daily rewards and blessings with you. I take Christ with me everywhere now.

Christ goes with me into my lectures and pharmacological research laboratory at the Georgetown Medical and Dental Schools, into my Sunday-school classroom and into every moment between. It is not easy, but no one must prove to me, a basic scientist, that Christ lives, by presenting unequivocal scientific facts or intellectual arguments. I *know* He is with me.

D.D.G.
WASHINGTON, D.C.

They tell of teenage terrors and triumphs.

"At fourteen . . . I was having an affair."

I will be a senior this coming year, and I am a teenager with problems—big problems! Many people would say that I should have no worries at all. I am a leader in my school; a cheerleader, class officer, class favorite, in all the clubs and organizations. But all this means nothing. Some people would give anything for what I've got, but I would give almost anything to be a very inconspicuous person.

As you said tonight, we grow up too fast and have no childhood. I was taking ballroom dancing at ten, going steady at twelve, drinking at fourteen, and also having an affair with my boy friend. At the ripe old age of seventeen, I'm thoroughly tired of living.

You're probably wondering if I come from a Christian family. Well, let's just say it's a church family. We go to the biggest, most beautiful Baptist church in town, with all the rest of the hypocrites, I might add. I might be

260

called a liar by some, but I really can't say that I know one true Christian.

I'm terribly bitter toward this world, but I know I have to live in it whether I like it or not. I know that God is the only one that can help me, but I've tried turning to Him. It seems my prayers just don't help, so pray for me, will you? Whatever you do don't send anything to my house. My mother will read my mail. Thank you for listening to my problems.

A.B.
LOUISIANA

"She didn't believe in Hell and all that junk."

I'm writing to say how glad I am that Billy Graham came to our city. I attended a Youth Night, and fervently wish that I had gone to one seven or eight years ago. If only more young people would listen! Some of the audience were treating it as a lark, and I wanted to grab them and make them listen. One girl said she didn't believe in "hell and all that junk." How I wanted to cry out: "There is! There is a hell! I lived there for five long and terrible years." Even though I was a teenager, I lived worse than any would believe, but a life that all too many teens now live because they are taught to laugh at God and morality. Everyone tells them about the joy, and no one tells about the pain and tragedy that must follow. I was lucky and found the right way out before I was destroyed.

But not all find redemption. Of my best friends in school, one was shot at sixteen by a policeman, one is serving twenty years for second-degree murder, one is in a mental hospital, and one killed herself when she became an unwed mother. They weren't raised in slums; they had every chance financially and educationally; but they were neglected spiritually.

Perhaps God has given me the chance to bring some light to these girls and others to come. Dr. Graham once said if he only helped one person to Christ his work would be worthwhile. Well, he has helped this person more than he'll ever know, and may God ever bless him for it.

MRS. J.S.
CALIFORNIA

"Our English teacher, a Jew, said listen."

I praise the Lord for your ministry and testimony. I'm a high school junior in Detroit. Our English teacher, who happens to be a Jew, made the assignment to all of her students and said listen to you. This was an answer to prayer. The Christians at school have been waiting for a chance to witness in full force. This may be the Lord's answer for you see this assignment was made for the night you discussed morals and teens. Praise the Lord!

J.R.
DETROIT, MICHIGAN

"You knocked some sense in my head."

Last night, June 1, you knocked some sense into my head. And maybe tomorrow night when you talk about sex you can help me some more.

I am sixteen and my father is a minister. I'm just starting to realize how sinful I really am. Thanks to you, I'm starting to act right.

M.L.
INDIANA

"You should talk to the Beatles."

I am a teenager and I like the Beatles. I think you should send someone to talk to them. I don't know whether they have given their lives to Christ but I know a talk with them would help them. This might even bring other teens to God. If they knew the Beatles had given their lives to Christ, they might start coming to the crusades.

L.K.
WINNIPEG, MANITOBA

"Something said that's you, boy!"

I know I've done wrong and I want to go straight. I'm a 16-year-old boy, I'm known as a wise guy, punk, and a few other things. Maybe I am, but when I listened to your last two sermons something started in me. Something said that's you boy! I'm talking to you!

We're moving into a new neighborhood and I feel I can start anew.

R.W.
ALBANY, NEW YORK

263

"Absolutely fantabulous."

My mother and I both watched the telecast of June second, and thought it was absolutely fantabulous!

I am a fourteen-year-old girl, who has made the decision.

K.M.
LOUISIANA

"I don't eat half the time."

I heard your first message the other night. I realized when you had finished the message that I did not not really know Christ. After the message I got on my knees and let Christ come into my heart. Even though I am a Sunday-school teacher I had never let Christ come into my heart before now.

This morning I read John 9:1-25. It tells of the story of a blind man being healed. As I read it this reminded me of my life. For so many years I was blind to Christ, but now I am able to see.

I am a college student. As you know it takes money to go to school. In fact I don't have enough to eat half the time. I know I can't send much, but I plan to send you 25¢ a week until I can send more.

F.B.
MISSISSIPPI

"I have lost four boy friends."

Greetings in our Savior's Name. I want to let you know how much your message of June 2d has done for me. I am a Christian, and I have lost four boy friends who also professed to be Christians, because I won't commit the sin of immorality.

I thank God for young men and women who are willing, in spite of sin and wickedness, to take their stand for God.

What your message has meant to me only eternity will reveal. I do covet your prayer. I have been a Christian for the past five years, and God has been wonderful to me.

G.W.
ONTARIO

They pledge their hearts and hands to God

"I enjoyed a smoke, a drink, and dancing."

I trained as a nurse in a London hospital, and spent all my time looking for entertainment. At twenty-one, I felt I needed sophistication; I enjoyed a smoke and a drink, and dancing.

Having seen most of the shows in town, I was at loose ends one day when a poster appeared on the board-

265

ings saying, "Hear Billy Graham." I concluded he must be a band leader because one of his companions had a trombone and the other was singing into a mike. The poster hit me from every street corner. "Thrill to the music . . ." it said.

At my hospital, some one had left a booklet saying, "This is the crisis time for revival." I read it and its message stuck in my head so I sneaked off one night to hear what it was all about.

As I arrived at Harringay, late, Billy Graham was saying, "You have come here tonight dissatisfied—looking for a purpose in life. You could leave here a new person." At the end, I rushed out, trying to evaluate the surge of spiritual desire that was overwhelming me. In my room, I fell crying on my knees and stayed there until daylight. Nobody knew of my experience but that morning a new life began. All my energy and enthusiasm were now directed to Christ. My friends soon despaired of getting me away from my "new craze."

Eight years later, God spoke to me about going to Brazil. I had never wanted to be a missionary, but by the end of the week I gave in. So I trained for three years, and sailed. I'm now in my fifth year of service. I live with one other girl in a small jungle town, and with medical and evangelistic outreach we seek to win people to Christ.

It would take a book to tell of our exciting adventures, and of how God has taken care of us through danger and loneliness. I have seen many miracles, but none greater than the change in my own life way back at Harringay in 1954.

A.K.S.

"For six years, I have been teaching."

When I was in Europe in World War II, God spoke to me at Bastogne during the Battle of the Bulge, and I vowed if I ever got home I would go to church regularly. I kept the vow, but never made a public profession of faith. The time never was right, so Satan said.

Mr. Graham came to St. Louis, and during the invitation, some unseen power lifted me from my seat and I found myself down front.

My experience with the Lord deepened; for six years I have been teaching thirteen-year-old boys in Sunday school and I go on visitation the third Thursday of each month.

P.A.
Missouri

"A sailor put a drug in my hand."

The eleventh day of February, 1957, 6 p.m., was the most important day and hour in the life of a nineteen-year-old young man, namely, me.

I had one outstanding desire, which was to be a syndicate crime leader in the city of Chicago.

A sailor put a drug in my hand, a drug which might well have led to my addiction. In planning a robbery I volunteered to carry a .45 automatic and to kill the night watchman, but the plan went awry. My last appearance in court resulted in a conviction for peddling stolen goods. I was sentenced to a term of one to six years.

267

While I was in my cell, a Christian visitor brought me a copy of your booklet, "The Seven Deadly Sins." To the best of my recollection, at that time the name of Jesus was foreign to me. I had never heard the plan of salvation. I did not know what it meant to be saved, or lost. But on that day, without a counselor or help of any kind, I cried out to God for help, and I found Christ.

Now, after having served fourteen months of my sentence, I am a freshman at Philadelphia College of Bible. I am with Youth for Christ, working with young people who are having problems with juvenile courts. My experiences with the Holy Spirit have been rich. The very men who tried to break my career as a juvenile delinquent are now writing me letters of recommendation. God bless you continually in your ministry.

G.F., Jr.
Pennsylvania

"I thought you might be good for a laugh."

Nine months ago I was ordained into the Baptist ministry, an event which ten years ago would have seemed as unlikely as my playing soccer in a Wembley Cup final. By an uncanny turn, my sixteenth year saw me on my way to hear America's new sensation, Dr. Billy Graham. Some other teenagers and I thought you might be good for a laugh.

But that visit to Harringay brought me face to face with God. To say that I was changed in a minute would be untrue. Yes, I had become a new person in God's sight, but that was only the beginning. As the excitement of that night wore off, I began to grasp more clearly what had happened. No longer was *self* the controlling factor, I discovered, for Christ had really invaded my personality and captured my heart.

REV. P.F.P.
KIRBY MUXLOE, LEICESTER

"I expected to see a raving charlatan."

The night the crusade opened, a Christian friend dragged me out to it. I had convinced myself that I would see a raving charlatan. I was curious to see how you would address a university audience and so I listened. Everything you said applied to me, and the sermon made a vivid impression on me. I now have the Bible verse you used, Hebrews 11:6, written on a piece of paper where I can always read it.

You told us to read the Gospels. After the service I went back to my room and found my Bible. (I had to wipe the dust off it before I opened it, but never again—I have read my Bible every day since.) That night I started reading the Bible, and Christ revealed himself to me. For the first time in my life I realized the significance of his sacrifice for us. I went back to the crusade and on the second-to-last night I went forward to rededicate myself to Christ. I was surprised to experience such a joy-filled moment.

As an officer cadet I am working with the Officers Christian Union, and I hope to go into the ministry when I finish my service in the Canadian army.

B.J.
KINGSTON, ONTARIO

"I asked twenty-two Girl Scouts to our home."

The three nights of watching you on television have done more for my fourteen-year-old daughter than all of my teaching and "preaching."

I am a Girl Scout leader of teenagers, and I asked twenty-two girls to our home to watch you on TV. I wish you could have seen their reaction and heard the fine discussion that followed. Bless you for your inspirational message to them—many of those girls found Christ. God grant that I may lead them on in Christ's footsteps.

(MRS.) R.C.
DERRY, PENNSYLVANIA

They tell of a change in their churches.

"Ninety-two percent remained faithful."

It has been more than two years since the crusade in Charlotte. Our church was committed without reservation to the total work: financially, with prayer helpers, ushers, advisers, choir members, counselors, and transportation. There were 108 decision cards referred to our church. The people were immediately contacted. Only one was not located.

After two years we have this report: thirteen moved their membership, six never came, two attend less than one service a month, and eighty-six are faithful members! We have the amazing record that 92 percent of those who went forward to make decisions remain faithful after two years.

This is a higher percentage of those remaining true to their decisions than in any other type of evangelism we have employed. "This is the Lord's doing, and it is marvelous in our eyes."

(Rev.) S.H.Z.
Charlotte, North Carolina

"I am preaching differently."

Somebody said to me, "What's happened to you? You are preaching differently!" Well, how can you help it when you have an experience inside you like this? The crusade is important because of the impact it has on people. Its benefit for a pastor is this: Jesus Christ is made uncompromisingly central.

Rev. L.P., late rector
New York City

271

"Never has our church been so packed."

How greatly blessed we were as individuals and as a congregation by the marvelous telecasts of the Los Angeles crusade!

The Sunday following, our congregation was so packed into our church that they filled the empty choir seats, the pastor's office, and even spilled over into the nursery. Never has our church been so packed, even on Easter Sundays. At least one family who had not been to church in many weeks testified to me as they left the service that they were there because of Billy Graham. We directly attribute this increase in attendance to the Lord's working through the crusade telecasts which were viewed so widely in this city.

A member of our choir whose work causes him to be on the road from 4:30 in the morning until late in the evening had retired from the choir several months ago. He returned this week. His reason—"As I watched Billy Graham the Lord made me realize that my work had to come second to my service to Him."

(REV.) F.M.B., JR.
BIRMINGHAM, ALABAMA

"We pastors are thrilled."

It was my privilege to serve as chairman for the counselor training classes in Lindsay in connection with the Fresno crusade. It was a thrill to see upwards of sixty persons of all denominations attend the classes to study God's Word and go on to counsel at the meetings last summer.

The best part is that Lindsay did not let its ministry stop when the crusade closed. The youth prayer groups that were started during the crusade were such a blessing to the young people that they continue to meet, with an average attendance of 150. The peak attendance was 200, with young people coming from all twenty-eight churches of Lindsay. At each meeting some find Christ as their Savior.

Let me tell you of another result. We now have two well supported Bible Clubs in Lindsay and Strathmore High Schools, with the attendance in the forties for both clubs.

This has spread further, to the Christian Business Men of Lindsay. The group meets every Friday morning from 6:30 to 7 a.m. for prayer (always praying for the Billy Graham team), then they have breakfast from 7:00 to 8:00. These men, stirred by the crusade, are faithfully serving the Lord in two road camps and sponsoring both Bible Clubs and a community sing. Their latest venture of faith is a City Mission and Sunday school.

(Rev.) T.D.W.
Lindsay, California

"Not one person has fallen back."

The immediate impact of the crusade upon our congregation was almost electrifying. Now, four years later, a more subdued atmosphere prevails. A more normal program has been resumed, but the fruits of crusade harvest remain. Not one person who was converted during the crusade, and joined our church, has fallen back. Most of them have shown remarkable evidences of growth, and a few are now among our most promising members. Our Sunday-school attendance is a full year ahead of the projected growth which was made before the crusade began. We have had to construct a $40,000 addition to our Sunday-school plant.

The fervid glow of crusade activity has faded, but the staunch results are evident in many lives, including especially a number of our high school young people who are now quietly preparing for missionary service.

(REV.) R.S., PASTOR
PALO ALTO, CALIFORNIA

"He was raising his pledge."

We're so grateful for your crusade. One man, Jeffrey, was a rather active churchman, but never a liberal giver. One night he attended your rally with me and served as an usher. When you gave the invitation to make a personal commitment, he did. I have never seen him so excited.

The next day Jeffrey told me, "I've been up all night thinking about some things that Billy Graham said. . . . I was so disturbed I couldn't sleep. About four o'clock I got up, awakened my wife and said to her, 'Honey, we're going to start tithing.' She got up, put on a pot of coffee, and we talked the rest of the night about God and what we were going to do. I've been a selfish man, watching some of you happy ones, and now I want to share the same joy."

T.M.
JACKSONVILLE, FLORIDA

They write of miracles, both large and small.

"I'd have told them they were crazy."

If people had told me ten years ago that I, a Jew, would be preaching about Jesus Christ, I'd have told them they were crazy. Yet God opens my mouth and I speak forth this Word. It was at the New York crusade that I received Christ.

E.H.F.,JR.
NEW YORK, NEW YORK

"Locked gates are nothing to the Lord."

I have been intending to write this letter ever since the 1963 crusade in Los Angeles. I've wanted to tell you of the miracle that took place in the stadium that last night.

As you know, it was filled to capacity and many people didn't get in. Our church chartered two buses and tried to leave early enough so that we could get in; but when we got there people were already being turned away. The bus I was on had all the children in it; so, not knowing what else to do, we returned to the bus. The children were getting restless and some of the men decided to go and see if they could find the others and tell them we were taking the bus and the children back to the church.

They returned after about ten minutes and told us that they had found one of the gates open and that we could get in. We gathered up the children and rushed back. We went in, and when we reached the top of the stairs two ushers told us the gate had been locked, but since we were in, to go as quietly as we could onto the field and sit down, because Mr. Graham was about to speak.

Another miracle came when you asked those who would accept Christ to stand. I was sitting there with my head bowed, praying, when I felt someone next to me move; I opened my eyes and looked up, thinking it was one of the children. To my surprise four of the adults in our group were going forward. Two were husband and wife, one was the mother of five children, and the fourth was a young Jewish woman.

Someone may have forgotten to lock that gate, but you'll never get us to believe it. We were there and we know that the gate was locked, but locked gates are nothing to the Lord. He'll open any gate to let in lost sheep.

(Mrs.) F.B.D.
California

276

"The family is now united."

A year ago we took into our home two foster girls, ages four and five, and shared with them the love of Christ. The oldest girl gave her heart to Christ, and daily the girls would pray that "Mama would ask Jesus into her heart."

The mother and father had been separated most of their married life. The father came occasionally to visit the children, and we were able to talk to him about Christ. He later went forward at an evangelistic meeting. What a wonderful change!

Then the mother started to come weekends. On the weekend that your crusade was televised, God arranged for us and the mother to visit the lady who had led me and my husband to Christ. Shortly after the invitation was given on the broadcast, our friend asked the young mother if she was right with the Lord. She burst into tears and in a few moments was led to a saving knowledge of Christ.

The mother quit her job in Seattle and was reunited with her husband. Five months later they received their children from the court. The family is now united in Christ and growing spiritually. How we thank God for answering prayer, and how we thank the Lord for using your broadcasts as a means of bringing this mother to Christ!

(Mrs.) M.D.T.
PORTLAND, OREGON

"Your sermon was meant for me."

Your sermon on Monday night was meant for me. I needed it to put me back on my knees. We have had a struggle in our last four years. My husband was laid off just eight years before retirement through no fault of his own. The company laid off sixty-six of them the same day and another seventy-five in a few weeks.

It is almost impossible for a man of that age to go out and get a job. People just look at you as if you are asking for the moon. Fortunately, he did get a job at about one-third of his former salary, but our problem was that we were looking back at what might have been. Your sermon helped me to feel we should be thankful for what we have, and to look ahead for better things. Enclosed find a small donation for your work.

(MRS.) L.MACD.

"I have held resentment for God for twelve years."

I have held resentment toward God for twelve years—ever since God took my dear mother, fifty-three years old, from us. I'd accept God and then toss him back out of my life. Last night after the third television crusade I turned my life completely over to him; I am saved now. I know nothing of how to live this new life, but I have a wonderful Savior for a friend.

(MRS.) M.L.
GREENVILLE, MICHIGAN

278

"Seventeen inmates have accepted Christ."

As a result of listening to your program from San Diego, California, seventeen inmates at the Elmira Reformatory have written me notes stating that they have responded to your message by accepting Christ as their personal Savior, and would like to receive the literature you are sending to new converts.

C.A.S.
PROTESTANT CHAPLAIN
ELMIRA, NEW YORK

"I feel a bit taller after watching you."

I feel compelled to write in response to your request asking whether your crusade on television is worthwhile. From the depths of my heart I say, yes.

Last spring we went as a family to a local church and heard a sermon entitled, "And With His Stripes We Are Healed." I had prayed many prayers but now realized I hadn't known to whom I was praying. The Bible was beyond my understanding. The pastor made an afternoon call to our home, and that evening, by myself, I accepted Christ.

Two days later I went forward at the altar call, and my husband, quite unexpectedly, made his stand for Christ by following me just a matter of moments later. It's as my husband said, he had gone to church before but

279

had never heard a sermon that explained that salvation was possible.

Happiness beyond description has been ours. Outwardly our lives have been altered and inwardly is a peace and purpose we have never known before. Our children, though young, have been amazed at the change Christ has made in our home.

We feel your telecast is important because you reach people who would not otherwise be reached, in their homes, where they will listen without fear of ridicule from others.

You strengthen us by letting God use you. I feel a bit taller after watching you, and look forward to standing up and being counted as a true disciple of Christ.

J. AND R.C.
GARDEN GROVE, CALIFORNIA

They send their love,
their thanks, their mite.

"I asked my daddy to go forward."

My mother and father and I were watching television when you came on. Mother insisted we watch you, so we did. Before I go on, I want to tell you I gave my life to God when I was nine. I was eight when you came to Little Rock.

I asked my daddy to go forward when the crowd went forward but he said, "Not this time, Ginny." When you finished your sermon, my daddy had tears in his eyes. My mother said, "I'd write to him, Don, please do!"

280

Well, in case he doesn't, I want to ask your prayers for my daddy.

I'm sending you this month's allowance, and would you please pray hard.

V.C.

"Thank you for standing by us."

I would like to thank Dr. Graham from the bottom of my heart for unknowingly serving as my pastor in Korea via "The Hour of Decision." Where I was located with a U.S. Military Police Company that's all a Christian had: his Bible and your radio program (over HLKX, Inchon).

Every place I've been in the world I've found "The Hour of Decision." On the way back from Korea (because of illness) I stayed overnight at a hospital in Texas, and while scanning the shortwave band on my radio I heard your message coming over HCJB from South America.

I have started that long physical climb back to health and I am aiming for the Vermont State Police.

I may be down, but I'm not out. Though I'm surrounded by darkness, I am in the light; for my Savior is with me. My greatest desire is to serve Him.

You always say on your radio program, "Thank you for your faithfulness in standing by us." Well, let me say, "Thank *you* for standing by *us* in our hours of greatest need."

B.K.H.
VALLEY FORGE GENERAL
HOSPITAL
PHOENIXVILLE, PENNSYLVANIA

Since his birth in 1902 in Montgomery City, Missouri, Curtis Mitchell has accumulated an impressive range of experience as writer, editor, administrator, and consultant to business and government.

His career as editor, which began in the print shop of a country weekly in Missouri, culminated in the 1930's with positions as vice-president and editorial director, first for Triangle Publications, then for the Dell Publishing Company.

Twice the government called upon Mr. Mitchell for special services. During World War II, he was awarded colonel's rank for his performance in the United States War Department's Bureau of Public Relations. Again in 1961, the Secretary of Labor and the Federal Aviation Agency obtained Mr. Mitchell's assistance.

Quite as diverse as his experience, Mr. Mitchell's intellectual interests encompass such subjects as religion, health, aviation, communism, science, and family life. His pen has kept pace with his mind. Mr. Mitchell's articles on health and science have appeared in a variety of magazines including *The Reader's Digest, The New York Times Sunday Magazine, Family Weekly,* and *Popular Science.*

Those Who Came Forward is the latest of four books the author has written, the others being *God in the Garden, Isometrics. . . . First Step Toward Fitness,* and *Fitness for the*

Whole Family, a work he wrote in collaboration with Dr. Paul Dudley White.

Mr. Mitchell promises to extend this list. Currently living and writing in a country home in Westport, Connecticut, he means to keep his pen as active as it has ever been, perhaps more so.